UNDERSTANDING
KNOWLEDGE ENGINEERING

ELLIS HORWOOD BOOKS IN INFORMATION TECHNOLOGY

General Editors: Dr JOHN M. M. PINKERTON, Information Technology
Consultant, J & H Pinkerton Associates, Esher, Surrey, and formerly
Manager of Strategic Requirements, International Computers Limited: and
V. A. J. MALLER, VM Associates; Visiting Professor in Computer Studies,
Loughborough University of Technology; formerly of Thorn EMI
Information Technology Ltd.
Consulting Editor: PATRICK HOLLIGAN, Department of Computer Studies,
Loughborough University of Technology

UNDERSTANDING KNOWLEDGE ENGINEERING

Editors

MICHAEL F. McTEAR
TERRY J. ANDERSON
both of Institute of Informatics
University of Ulster at Jordanstown, Northern Ireland

Contributors
Terry Anderson, Edwin P. Curran, Lindsey Ford, Mike Greenwell,
Frank Hickman, Khalid P. Ishaq, Brendan McGee, Michael McTear,
Felix Schmidt, Jason Trenouth and Masoud Yazdani

ELLIS HORWOOD LIMITED
Publishers · Chichester

Halsted Press: a division of
JOHN WILEY & SONS
New York · Chichester · Brisbane · Toronto

First published in 1990 by
ELLIS HORWOOD LIMITED
Market Cross House, Cooper Street,
Chichester, West Sussex, PO19 1EB, England
The publisher's colophon is reproduced from James Gillison's drawing of the ancient Market Cross, Chichester.

Distributors:

Australia and New Zealand:
JACARANDA WILEY LIMITED
GPO Box 859, Brisbane, Queensland 4001, Australia

Canada:
JOHN WILEY & SONS CANADA LIMITED
22 Worcester Road, Rexdale, Ontario, Canada

Europe and Africa:
JOHN WILEY & SONS LIMITED
Baffins Lane, Chichester, West Sussex, England

North and South America and the rest of the world:
Halsted Press: a division of
JOHN WILEY & SONS
605 Third Avenue, New York, NY 10158, USA

South-East Asia
JOHN WILEY & SONS (SEA) PTE LIMITED
37 Jalan Pemimpin # 05–04
Block B, Union Industrial Building, Singapore 2057

Indian Subcontinent
WILEY EASTERN LIMITED
4835/24 Ansari Road
Daryaganj, New Delhi 110002, India

© **1990 M. McTear and T.J. Anderson/Ellis Horwood Limited**

British Library Cataloguing in Publication Data
Understanding knowledge engineering. —
(Ellis Horwood series in information technology).
1. Expert systems
I. McTear, Michael, *1943–* II. Anderson, Terry J.
006.3'3

Library of Congress Card No. 89–24493

ISBN 0–7458–0634–1 (Ellis Horwood Limited — Library Edn.)
ISBN 0–7458–0802–6 (Ellis Horwood Limited — Student Edn.)
ISBN 0–470–21646–8 (Halsted Press)

Printed in Great Britain by Hartnolls, Bodmin

Contents

Contributors

Terry J. Anderson, Department of Information Systems, Institute of Informatics, University of Ulster

Edwin P. Curran, Department of Computer Science, Institute of Informatics, University of Ulster

Lindsey Ford, Department of Computer Science, University of Exeter

Mike Greenwell, Knowledge Engineer, Oxford

Frank R. Hickman, Touche Ross Management Consultants, London

Khalid P. Ishaq, British Telecom Research Laboratories, Martlesham Heath

Brendan McGee, Generics Software Ltd, Dublin

Michael F. McTear, Department of Information Systems, Institute of Informatics, University of Ulster

Felix A. Schmidt, Department of Civil Engineering and Transport, University of Ulster

Jason Trenouth, Department of Computer Science, University of Exeter

Masoud Yazdani, Department of Computer Science, University of Exeter

Introduction

Michael F. McTear and Terry J. Anderson

Expert systems have often been defined as programs that use knowledge to solve problems. For this reason they are also referred to as knowledge-based systems. But what does it mean when we say that a program uses knowledge to solve a problem in contrast to the data used by conventional programs? How does knowledge differ from data? What sort of knowledge can we put into a computer program? Where does the knowledge come from, how is it stored and how is it used to solve the sorts of problems that usually require human expertise?

The answers to these questions lie at the heart of knowledge engineering. The knowledge engineer elicits knowledge about a particular problem — such as how to invest wisely on the stock-market — and represents this knowledge in a computer program in such a way that it can be used on subsequent occasions to solve similar problems.

However, knowledge engineering involves much more than this. In addition to solving problems, expert systems need to be able to explain how they reached their conclusions. They also need to be able to explain their reasoning in such a way that the human user can understand how the problem was solved and verify the validity of the conclusions.

In contrast then to conventional programs, knowledge-based systems use knowledge acquired from human experts to solve problems, give advice and explain their reasoning. They also differ from conventional programs in the following respects: the problems they solve are often unstructured and ill-defined; the knowledge they employ to solve these problems tends to take the form of facts combined with rules of thumb rather than well-structured data combined with algorithms; and there is usually an emphasis on the need for an intelligent and adaptive user interface which not only enables the system to explain and justify what it does but facilitates communication with the user in the acquisition and restructuring of knowledge.

The methodology of knowledge engineering has developed considerably over the past few years. The aim of the present book is to document the current state of the art in knowledge engineering, examine techniques which are currently available, set out the principles that support the design of knowledge-based systems, and explore the potential for future developments. But before moving on to these issues, it will be helpful to show how knowledge engineering is distinctive, and, in particular, how its methodology differs from that of conventional programming, as embodied in the discipline of software engineering.

KNOWLEDGE ENGINEERING AND SOFTWARE ENGINEERING — A COMPARISON

The traditional software development life-cycle of software engineering consists of a sequence of distinct stages through which a project must pass. The life-cycle begins with (1) a written statement of requirements. This is analysed to provide (2) clear and detailed specifications which are the basis for (3) the design process. In this phase the overall system architecture is established by the stepwise refinement process, in which large tasks are repeatedly decomposed, resulting in a hierarchy of self-contained components which address tasks of a more manageable size. Algorithms and data structures for these components are then developed. The next stage, (4) program implementation, entails a comparatively straightforward translation of the design into program code. The program is then (5) tested against the specifications, and bugs are fixed. This usually involves going back to amend flaws in earlier phases, so there are feedback loops among the stages. The final phase, (6) maintenance, begins after system delivery and continues during the lifetime of the software.

Fundamental to the success of software engineering are clear requirements and precise specifications. The problems which the system must solve are identified in iron-clad detail. The distinction between correct and incorrect input data which the system must process is unambiguously defined, and the range of processing options is usually quite small. From the start, then, the task is completely known and all eventualities can be allowed for.

System specification represents a much greater challenge in knowledge engineering because the problems it addresses are considerably more complex. For knowledge-based systems it is impractical to suggest that all possible combinations of input could be anticipated or that all possible explanations could be prespecified. Prototyping has become the dominant development methodology because it provides a mechanism for identifying software requirements. Repeatedly cycling through four steps — requirements gathering, quick design, implementation and evaluation — enables the developer to understand with increasing precision what needs to be done.

Stepwise refinement in software engineering provides very clear guidance to the designer on how to structure the software. Also available are tried and tested control structures and a wealth of proven data structures. No comparable unifying design approach would seem possible in knowledge engineering because knowledge varies so greatly according to problem domains. Many of the control and knowledge representation structures have a short history, and their strengths and weaknesses may not be fully apparent.

Associated with each stage in the software development life-cycle are one or more well-established notations, and the construction of software proceeds by methodical transformation from one notation to the next: from English requirements to specifications in data flow diagrams or logic, from software designs in structure charts and pseudocode, to program code. This is of great assistance to the designer, allowing him to start from a high level of abstraction and refine it to a concrete implementation. The absence in knowledge engineering of an equivalent set of standard notations, except the implementation language, makes it more difficult for the designer to envisage the overall system structure.

The products of software engineering are rigorously tested against the initial specifications. This allows results to be classified as correct or incorrect, although ensuring that all paths through the software are checked still represents a significant challenge. The less firm specifications associated with knowledge engineering, coupled with greater system complexity, mean that comparable thoroughness in testing is not viable. At best, successful processing of test cases, as judged by a domain expert, can inspire confidence — but never certainty — in a system's adequacy and reliability.

Over the past few years, knowledge-engineering methodology has borrowed and adapted much from its 20-year-old elder brother, software engineering. This trend seems likely to continue (see, for example, Chapter 2), paving the way for the widespread integration of conventional and knowledge-based software. The potential for products which combine the strengths of established systems, such as databases or spreadsheets, with expert level manipulation of information is enormous.

ABOUT THIS BOOK

Knowledge engineering refers to the process of acquiring knowledge from a human expert and shaping it in such a way that it can be used efficiently in a knowledge-based system. As we see it, knowledge engineering can be divided into several distinct components: expert system project management, expert system design, knowledge elicitation, knowledge programming and user interface design. These components are reflected in the chapters of this book. In addition, the knowledge engineer needs to consider what tools to use for building an expert system.

Chapter 1 provides a general introduction to the question of the management of expert system projects. In this chapter Yazdani brings out the differences between conventional software development and that of expert systems, outlining a series of phases which an expert system project should take. Essentially he recommends a cyclical approach, which is a kind of controlled development. Expert systems are more flexible than conventional software and can permit the introduction of complexity during the development period, whereas this is not possible using algorithmic techniques. However, as Yazdani points out, an expert system project may involve a mix of traditional data processing with expert systems and artificial intelligence elements. What is to be avoided is what he refers to as 'creep' — either away from a heuristic approach or towards an algorithmic solution — since 'creeping' away from expert system methods means creeping away from their benefits.

In Chapter 2 Hickman takes up in greater detail the issue of specifying a methodology for the construction of knowledge-based systems. The proposed methodology does not differ substantially from that of the conventional software development life-cycle model except that it involves more complex problems, such as dealing with knowledge about the data and its use. Hickman proposes a modelling approach to expert systems development which contrasts with the more usual method of knowledge extraction, prototyping and incremental development. He illustrates this approach with an example of a system under development for use in decision support for the marketing-planning process, showing how development progresses through a series of models. The life-cycle model can also be thought of as a model for project management and control.

Knowledge acquisition refers to the process of eliciting knowledge from an expert with reference to a particular problem domain. This stage is often seen as one of the more problematic aspects of knowledge engineering. First it is necessary to select a problem which will be potentially amenable to knowledge-based problem solving. Then an expert has to be found who can provide information about the sorts of knowledge required to solve the problem. Eliciting knowledge from a human expert and then transforming this knowledge into an implementable form demands a high degree of expertise, and as yet there are few established principles and techniques as compared with traditional software development. For this reason the knowledge acquisition stage has been referred to as a 'bottle-neck' in expert systems development. The problems of knowledge elicitation are the subject of Chapter 3, in which Greenwell evaluates a variety of approaches in terms of their psychological validity as well as their practical utility.

There are two aspects to knowledge programming: how knowledge is to be represented in a computer program and what sorts of tools are available for the representation and utilization of knowledge. A variety of different knowledge representation techniques have been used in expert systems, and those which are typically found in commercially available expert system development tools — including production rules, predicate calculus, seman-tic nets and frames — are described and critically evaluated by McGee in Chapter 4. Two types of knowledge are distinguished: heuristic knowledge (or 'rules of thumb'), which encapsulates the problem-solving skills acquired by the expert as a result of experience; and descriptive knowledge, which refers to the knowledge relevant to the problem domain.

In Chapter 5 Ishaq examines the sorts of tools — such as expert system shells — which have become available for knowledge programming and outlines the questions to be asked with regard to the selection of a particular type of tool. The advantages and disadvantages of the knowledge represen-tation formalisms described in Chapter 4 are outlined in relation to expert system tools. Facilities for developing a user interface with debugging and explanation facilities as well as external interfaces — for example, to large-scale databases — are discussed. The choice of a particular tool — whether a language, a shell or a knowledge-engineering tool — requires consideration of the degree of flexibility required for the system as well as the ease of development and implementation of the system.

It is often helpful when discussing knowledge engineering to look at an actual case study describing the design and development of an expert system. In Chapter 6 Curran and Schmidt take up and illustrate many of the points raised in the preceding chapters, including the contrast between the methodologies of knowledge-based programming and conventional software development. They show how they developed an expert system for ship evaluation and design using a particular knowledge-engineering tool (Xi Plus). Thus this chapter provides a practical demonstration of the utility of a knowledge-engineering tool for the design of an actual expert system. At the same time various enhancements are introduced — including a link with a graphics package to assist the designer and an interface to a conventional programming language to allow routines to be written to aid numerical optimization.

One aspect of knowledge engineering which has tended to be overlooked in the past, but which is increasingly attracting attention, concerns the design of the user interface. As was pointed out earlier, this aspect is especially important for expert systems since part of their functionality is concerned with providing explanations of their problem solving in terms amenable to the user as well as interacting with the user to elicit information necessary for the problem-solving process. For this reason we have included two chapters on issues concerned with the user interface. In Chapter 7 Anderson describes the general dialogue principles involved in the design of the user interface, while in the final chapter Trenouth and Ford discuss a variety of approaches to user modelling.

User modelling refers to the technology of enabling the computer to adapt to the requirements of individual users. A detailed classification scheme of different dimensions of user modelling gives some insight into the complexity of what is involved in attempting to make the computer more sensitive to the various needs, interests and preferences of users. The second part of the chapter describes a project for knowledge-based engineering training (KBET) which incorporates knowledge about the user as an essential component as well as a practical illustration of many other knowledge-engineering issues raised in earlier chapters.

Knowledge engineering is a rapidly evolving discipline which depends on advances in theoretical areas such as artificial intelligence and cognitive science. Already there is talk of a second generation of expert systems in which more advanced techniques and principles are to be applied. There is no doubt that we will see many new developments in knowledge-engineering theory and practice over the next few years. The chapters in this book indicate the current state of the art as well as suggesting some ways forward.

1

Managing expert system projects

Masoud Yazdani

1.1 INTRODUCTION

When a project manager plans the development of new accounting or process-monitoring software, he is supported by a general body of knowledge of how similar projects have worked out in the past. The programmers on the project may have been involved in similar jobs, and the project is further assisted by a number of project management methodologies which are being successfully used in the development of complex software.

However, the development of an expert system is a relatively new field and so it is not surprising that there is no commonly accepted methodology for approaching a new project. Each developer of an expert system is a pioneer unsupported by any knowledge of what lies ahead, with not even the comfort of knowing that there is an end to the project!

The time and budgetary constraints mean that it is important to be able to plan a project and monitor progress, and to structure the work so as to take account of the peculiarities of expert systems.

Through my experience at Exeter University and Expert Systems International Ltd some primary principles were noted. It is not felt that a methodology in the sense of a rigid set of predefined steps is appropriate, but that the guidelines drawn up offer the flexibility and generality required.

1.2 CYCLICAL DEVELOPMENT

The one-shot approach (specification to implementation) of conventional software development is not appropriate to expert system technology. In most cases the discovery of the specification in an expert system project is itself a problem which needs to be solved empirically. The use of a throw-away prototype simplifies the process a great deal.

The project could be undertaken in at least five phases. These phases constitute a sophisticated workplan, adopted in response to the demands of expert systems technology. It is of prime importance to explore requirements and feasibility, and to construct the basis of progress monitoring, at the outset of the project.

1.2.1 Preliminary phase

In this phase what is needed are a feasibility study and consideration of how to integrate the projected system into a broader computational context. What must also be considered is the role of the user from the outset.

The detailed parts of the preliminary phase require explorations in depth of particular topics, and interviews with individuals. The most important outputs of this stage are statements of the 'project objectives' and a 'statement of requirements' for the system. The requirements are expectations from the system. The objectives include the development of a system, but commonly include some other objectives such as the acquisition of experience on the part of corporate departments, piloting or feasibility demonstration for other projects, and the like.

It is necessary early in the project to obtain a set of sample consultations, both for technical purposes and to assist in monitoring progress. These 'test cases' should as closely as possible take the form of consultations exactly as they will be supported by the projected system, which will be tried on the system at the close of each phase in the cycle. It is usually worth including the process of obtaining the information as part of the knowledge engineering in the preliminary phase since this may well provide information on feasibility issues, including the availability of the expertise which the system is to incorporate.

1.2.2 Prototype phase

The 'throw-away' prototype is not required to be a fully operational system, but rather to act as a proof of the concept and to demonstrate various specific features to the experts and the users in order to motivate a detailed process of knowledge elicitation. This will greatly increase the level of knowledge in the system since most human experts find it easier to criticize a working system.

Detailed decisions about planning this phase are among the outputs of the preliminary phase, but in most cases it is appropriate to provide a screen demonstration of the intended system early on in this phase. This 'demonstration system' serves to confirm the results of system requirements and to clarify the final objective.

In most projects it is possible to find a ready-made shell which will support a worthwhile knowledge acquisition effort to start with, and thereby delay infrastructure work until the main phase. This is normally advisable in order to avoid an overcrowded prototyping phase.

1.2.3 Main phase

This is basically the main part of the project concerned with the development of the actual system. This new system is developed with a great deal of understanding based on the mistakes made while developing the prototype.

The main phase involves the eternal loop of 'testing', 'debugging' and 'refining' the system until it is satisfactory. Therefore this phase should be viewed as a number of phases in its own right.

1.2.4 Evaluation
Although each phase of the development includes an evaluation of the system by experts, an independent evaluation of the system needs to be made with the potential user population.

1.2.5 Maintenance
The final phase of the project will involve end-user training and keeping the system running to a satisfactory level.

1.3 KNOWLEDGE ANALYSIS APPROACH TO EXPERT SYSTEM DEVELOPMENT

In the previous section we argued that the 'one-shot' approach of conventional software development is unsuitable for expert systems. It is not possible to separate the specification from the implementation easily. Finding the specification is sometimes difficult and the use of a prototype may help. Sometimes the specification forms the greater part of the work and at other times it is the specification which is the problem.

Even data-processing people are finding the one-shot approach tricky, and prototyping is becoming popular in many parts of the software industry. Expert systems need a cyclical development, which is a kind of controlled prototyping. The important point is the 'control'.

Many people get carried away and think that prototyping is an end in itself. Some are influenced by the experimental programming style of the artificial intelligence community. However, if expert systems are to be developed into robust pieces of software, under clear project management disciplines, a way needs to be found to make the 'control' more explicit.

One form of useful discipline is called knowledge analysis. This involves finding a way to record the knowledge before the implementation begins, which means a partitioning of the knowledge elicitation effort from the implementation.

There are other reasons why the analysis approach is important. The implementation formalism may need to be changed a number of times in the life of a project, and one does not want to go back and carry out a new round of interviews just because the implementation formalism has been changed.

This in turn means that a form of 'intermediate representation' has to be found which can be used to record the knowledge gathered during the elicitation phase. The paper version of the system would be built in a complete fashion before starting to write any of it in a knowledge representation language (KRL).

Some of the intermediate representations normally used are:

● structured English
● ATNs
● production rules
● flow charts
● task decomposition trees
● semantic networks
● computer-aided elicitation methods
● concept editors
● hypertext

1.3.1 Management of cycles

The analysis approach can be used as a way of controlling the number of cycles involved and what is done in each one. A prototype, called 'the first cut', may help in the elicitation process. However, it can be assumed that enough knowledge is gathered so we do not need to go back to the experts too many times during the main phase of the project.

Each cycle of the main phase would attempt to implement a bigger portion of the knowledge as written up in the intermediate representation. In this way the intermediate representation acts as the equivalent of a specification in expert system development. The difference is that it need not be as cut and dried as the one-shot approach. If more elicitation is needed during the main phase, this can be done.

Each cycle would follow the same set of steps below:

(1)   cycle definition
(2)   infrastructure design
(3)   infrastructure implementation and debugging
(4)   knowledge base redesign
(5)   knowledge base implementation
(6)   evaluation
(7)   knowledge base debugging
(8)   decision to finish
(9)   documentation
(10) demonstration.

Therefore the system is incrementally developed with as many cycles as needed (or as many as can be afforded!). Each cycle begins with a set of objectives and ends with a demonstration. There is a certain amount of room for manoeuvre, but good practice will reduce the amount of toing and froing.

Fig. 1.1 shows how different tasks of knowledge engineering are performed within the various phases of the project. As can be seen, a move is made a little down the list each time, redoing some steps. Although a scientific methodology of the controlled cyclical development does not exist, many project managers have mastered the art of this and hopefully a little of the flavour of this art is communicated in this paper.

Task	Prelim.	First	Main1	Main2 ...
1. Project selection	*			
2. Feasibility study	*	(*)		
3. Project planning	*	*	(*)	
4. User identification	*	*	(*)	
5. Knowledge elicitation	(*)	*	(*)	
6. Knowledge analysis		*	*	(*)
7. Choice of tools		*	*	*
8. Coding the knowledge		*	*	*
9. Validation with experts		(*)	*	*
10. Maintenance procedure design		(*)	*	*
11. Evaluation with users			*	(*)
12. Maintenance				

Task	Main*	Eval.	Maintenance
1. Project selection			
2. Feasibility study			
3. Project planning			
4. User identification			
5. Knowledge elicitation			
6. Knowledge analysis			
7. Choice of tools	(*)		
8. Coding the knowledge	*		
9. Validation with experts	*	(*)	
10. Maintenance procedure design	(*)	*	(*)
11. Evaluation with users		*	*
12. Maintenance			*

Fig. 1.1 — Different tasks at various phases of a knowledge-engineering project.

1.4 BENCH TESTING

With traditional computing systems it is normal to think of bench testing as a process well near the end of the development cycle. However, most successful expert system projects pay attention to it at a very early stage. In fact test cases play 'a critical role in the development as well as the evaluation of most expert systems.

The common component of all expert systems is that they incorporate judgemental and analytical aspects of some form of human expertise. The significant aspect of this expertise is that its content is not clearly discernible at the outset.

'Knowledge elicitation' techniques (see e.g. Greenwell 1988) are concerned with elucidating this expertise and expressing it as an operational computer program. However, almost all these techniques rely upon the refinement and continuous modification of the emerging knowledge.

This contrasts with traditional computing systems, where development methodologies seek to eliminate, or at least minimize, the feedback from later stages to earlier ones. The important point, however, is to recognize that this feedback is an essential part of developing an expert system.

1.4.1 Test case sets

It is necessary early on in the project to obtain a set of sample 'test cases'. These should take the form of consultations between the expert and the user exactly as will be supported by the projected system. Each test case should consist of case details, intermediate consultations, the entire reasoning process, the conclusions and the justifications offered. They should range from trivial cases to those which would be considered too difficult for the computer system.

The cases must be typical situations with regular solutions. Unusual situations may mislead the development team. They must be realistic. Whilst looking for test cases, they need to be drawn from the workstream by observational or protocol analysis methods as much as possible, otherwise the selection of cases can easily become biased, rationalized or fictitious.

The set of test cases must comprise a suitable size. The number needed depends on the project but should be at least 8 to 10 within a good range of difficulty. The reasoning path of cases should include both the successful routes as well as any false starts or failures.

1.4.2 The advantages

Using a suite of test cases from the outset helps with making informed judgements at the feasibility stage of a project. They also play a major role in monitoring the progress. Moreover, such test cases help in the initial stages when it is hard to think of ways of getting started. One can start by writing a system which supports some of the test cases and the system can then be generalized in such a way that it could solve other similar problems.

At the end of each phase of the development cycle the system should be tested on the entire test set and the results noted. It is easy when fixing the system to cope with a difficult case to 'over-complicate' its reasoning so that it falls down on easier ones. The use of test cases, therefore, also acts as a warning sign when new modifications lead to overall regress in the performance of the system.

1.4.3 The disadvantages

There is obviously a danger of 'over-fitting' the system to the test cases. It is all too easy to 'fix' the system in such a way that it works well for the known problems but may fail on all other cases. If the system was meant to deal with a known set of cases it would have been a candidate for an algorithmic approach. The more the generality of the knowledge-based approach is shied away from, the more its benefits will be lost.

The circular nature of using test cases, both as a development tool and a bench testing tool, should be noted and any potential hazards guarded against. Whilst the use of test cases facilitates evaluation as an integral part of the development cycle, it will not eradicate the need for 'blind' validation with human experts and, ultimately, evaluation with normal users of the system.

1.4.4 Evaluation

It is important to note that there are three independent groups which all need to be involved in the evaluation of the system. The existence of a set of test cases in advance should primarily assist the system builders. The human experts are by nature sceptical of the system and would find it easy to criticize the system in the early stages. Nevertheless, they tend to build a 'hidden' test set of their own in order to put the system through its paces.

The fact that they normally fix on a set, however hidden, means that their effectiveness should not be totally relied upon. At best the experts validate that the system contains the expertise that they have communicated to the system builders.

The most important group is the potential user population. Unfortunately, in practice, this category is mostly ignored, making expert systems particularly prone to user rejection. It has become clear that users' expectations, level of understanding and abilities have to be considered from the outset in the development cycle. If possible a sample representative of the user population should be part of the development team, whilst 'blind' testing of the system by fresh 'unprimed' users should act as a safeguard.

1.5 FLEXIBILITY

Perhaps the key technical feature of expert systems is the flexibility with which changes (particularly those of an unforeseen nature and those that radically increase complexity) can be made to the system. This feature justifies the incremental development strategy of expert system projects.

Plotting cost against complexity in Fig. 1.2, we see that traditional DP and ES solutions show different curves.

The one-shot specification to implementation of traditional DP limits the complexity of a single specification. The complexity limit of the DP solution is specific to the algorithm adopted. During the development period the complexity grows very rapidly and is hard to control.

Until the complexity limit is reached, the algorithmic solution is cheaper. Therefore there is a temptation throughout an expert system project to revert to cheaper algorithmic techniques.

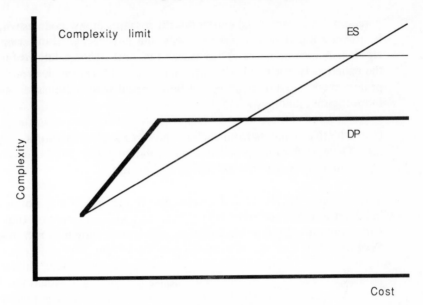

Fig. 1.2 — Plotting cost against complexity.

However, after the complexity limit is reached, any unexpected changes to the system will require a return to first principles and building an almost new system with a new curve.

On the other hand, the ES solution would grow in complexity at a steady rate. This proves a handicap in the early stages of a project. However, the absence of a limit to the complexity offers dividends in the form of flexibility.

1.5.1 The hybrid nature of expert systems

Expert systems cannot be seen in isolation from other forms of computer software. The best way to view them is as a bridge between the traditional DP and avant-garde AI.

DP applications rely on a simple match between a problem and an algorithmic solution to it. AI systems on the other hand would be ready to search a large space of possible solutions. In between these two there is what Clancey (1985) has called heuristic classification. Basically this means that although a simple match is not carried out, open-ended searches are avoided through heuristic short-cuts known by a human expert.

On the surface this seems straightforward. A good ES application is one that is clearly somewhere in the middle of that spectrum. However, in reality every ES application is in fact made out of parts of the whole of the spectrum of the following areas of knowledge:

(1)   Strictly procedural
(2)   Analytical and judgemental
(3)   Highly creative.

A reasonably complicated expert system contains many modules which can be best developed in an algorithmic way: the data storage, the user interface, etc. It may also be necessary to search for some of the solutions for which the expert may not be able to offer short-cuts. Therefore an expert system project needs to have a strategy of how to deal with these issues, as in the following methodology:

(1)   Identify elements from each of the three knowledge areas.
(2)   Develop fixes for procedural and creative parts.
(3)   Elicit analytical and judgemental expertise.

The exact mix of DP, AI and ES elements in the project may not be known in advance. However, most ES projects start with an intention that the ES part should dominate the effort. The mix is best shown as a triangle (see Fig. 1.3).

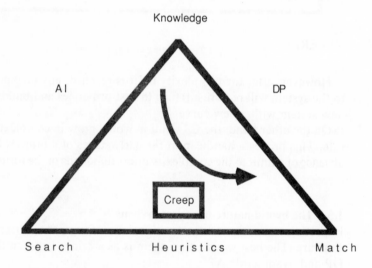

Fig. 1.3 — Creeping away from the ES approach.

1.5.2 Creep

During the lifetime of a project a number of influences combine pressures to creep away from a heuristic approach; first towards an open-ended AI approach and ultimately towards an algorithmic solution.

The problem starts with the project team's over-confidence: 'Why should I ask the expert when I can write a smart program which finds the solution?'. There is a great temptation to ignore the expert's advice and work out a new and apparently better way of doing things. However, after a while things do not work out, costs start mounting up and time gets short.

The most obvious pressure to 'creep' is the cost associated with the knowledge-engineering effort, coupled with the greater familiarity of most programmers with algorithmic languages. Common understanding and ease of communication between team members also lead to them leaning towards traditional methods.

Ultimately the fact that traditional methods require less effort at the design and implementation stages means that 'creep' becomes a major problem in an expert system development project. The more powerful the knowledge representation methods chosen, the stronger the pressure to creep becomes. However, creeping away from ES methods means creeping away from their benefits. If the intention was to build a traditional system, this should have been decided upon at the outset. The temptation to 'creep' should be resisted.

Creep can be pre-empted by choosing to implement one part of the system by an algorithmic method in one development cycle and rewriting it in a knowledge-based method in a later cycle. The good news is that once 'creep' is understood it can be foreseen and avoided. Furthermore, creep can be spotted and corrected in retrospect.

REFERENCES

Clancey, W. J. (1985) Heuristic Classification, *Artificial Intelligence* **27**, 289–350

Cupello, J. J., & Mishelevich, D. (1988) Managing prototype knowledge/expert system projects. *Communications of the ACM* **31** 534–541

Davies, P. (1985) Planning an expert system. *Proceedings of the First International Expert Systems Conference on Learned Information* pp. 243–261

Greenwell, M. (1988) *Knowledge engineering for expert systems.* Ellis Horwood, Chichester

2

Building intelligent knowledge-based systems

Frank R. Hickman

2.1 INTRODUCTION

This chapter is concerned with the construction of intelligent knowledge-based systems (IKBS). There are, however, problems for an author at this early stage in the development of such systems — by all accounts we cannot build them yet! Many are the definitions and descriptions of human intelligence. Many are the definitions and descriptions of systems aimed at simulating human intelligence. Many are the arguments for and against whether we can or even will be able to build such systems. However, what is certain is that today's technology enables us to build systems that demonstrate aspects of intelligent behaviour. They may 'learn' or they may make intelligent-looking decisions, but what is very clear is that these systems require knowledge in order to perform. Developments in the 1970s have shown us the power of this approach — the use of a knowledge base — and the advent of the so-called expert systems which represent the front-end of IKBS development. Fig. 2.1 shows an idealized knowledge-based systems structure.

In this chapter we will be indicating ways in which these systems may be built — in fact, putting forward a particular approach to system construction. This methodology, theoretically, should enable the construction of such systems, but such is the state of current technology and expertise that we would like to draw the distinction between IKBS, KBS and expert systems. True expert systems are IKBS. Today's technology is about KBS and it is these systems that will be discussed.

The term knowledge-based is used rather than expert system because it is required to include those systems which do not have the ability to truly learn, i.e. make new inferences from internally constructed data/information/knowledge. The boundary between automatically maintained (updating) knowledge-based systems and true expert systems is admittedly fuzzy.

Central to the construction process is the role of the knowledge engineer and this is also discussed and emphasized throughout the chapter. Also, in order to clarify certain aspects of the system-building methodology, we have

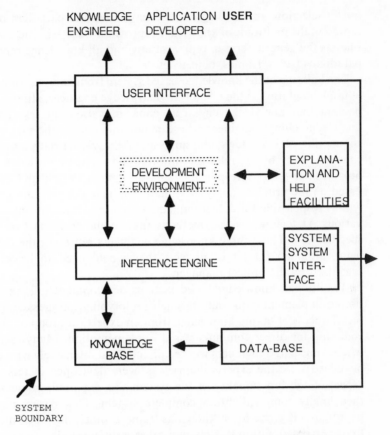

Fig. 2.1 — Typical knowledge-based system architecture.

used the domain of marketing planning as a platform for discussion. This should not present too many problems since most of the domain-dependent terms are readily understood.

The procedural role of the knowledge engineer in the development of the system is indicated in Fig. 2.2. Here again we are concerned mainly with a human–system interaction, although it is highly likely that many future systems might involve system–system interaction where the knowledge to be engineered is not residual in any one expert at all!

The diagram emphasizes the role of the knowledge engineer as the interface between the human expert and the system being developed. His/her role is typically one of extraction, amendment, refinement and

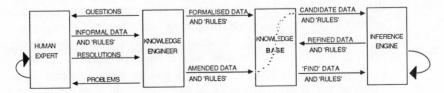

Fig. 2.2 — Knowledge Engineer — System Interchange.

finally selection. In the diagram, we have used the paradigm of 'rules' to represent the multitude of knowledge representations — i.e. here we shall use rules as the generic term to represent any and all knowledge representation paradigms (rules, frames, objects, etc.).

The building of the knowledge-based system from analysis, through design to implementation is the task of the knowledge engineer, although it should be said that knowledge engineers come in various guises. There is the knowledge elicitor/engineer whose major role entails the preparation and conducting of interviews, the analysis of the verbal data and its concatenation with other relevant information. The knowledge engineer/ programmer will be responsible for the system design and construction based on the previous analysis. Finally, we have the programmer/engineer who is responsible for actual implementation and must be able to code the various AI techniques and methods that should form part of the design specification. These three knowledge engineers represent the development team, although for larger projects they would need to be 'cloned' and organized by the project manager.

'Traditional' knowledge-based systems development follows the extraction-to-implementation route through prototyping, progressing by a piecemeal process of taking knowledge from an expert (or group of experts) and codifying for direct computer-based implementation. Many early systems, where knowledge engineers worked directly and intensively with the expert, or indeed were the experts themselves, were developed in this way. Each aspect of the functionality of the system was explored, implemented and then finally compiled into a complete system. This system development paradigm has come to be known as 'rapid prototyping'. The methodology to be expanded within this chapter takes a different viewpoint.

2.2 THE MODELLING VIEWPOINT

A more general view than that expressed above considers expertise as a distributed phenomenon. This means that knowledge which manifests itself as expertise in a particular domain in the functioning of a particular individual actually exists independently of that individual. The essence of this world-view is that this knowledge may be captured and codified and the associated behaviour replicated by a computer system. The importance of this idea is that knowledge acquisition — that part of the knowledge engineer's task which involves 'acquiring' the knowledge — is governed by a modelling paradigm rather than an action paradigm of extraction (from the expert). Thus knowledge engineering, and in particular knowledge acquisition, becomes a model-driven process whereby the engineer attempts to model the 'real' world, leading to eventual realization through some artefact — a computer system in our case. In fact this viewpoint lends credence to the supposition that knowledge-based systems creation and development is an engineering activity whereby a modelling language is devised to map from the observed behaviour to the artefact. Traditional

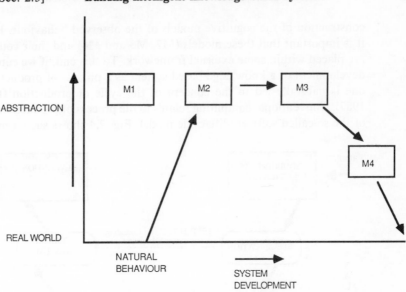

Fig. 2.3 — Model-driven system development.

engineering uses mathematics as this description language while knowledge engineering has, as such, no formalized language. The use of modelling and its function are illustrated in Fig. 2.3 (Hayward 1987).

It is important at this stage to understand this creative process. Model M1 would be an abstraction of behavioural realism and as such would only capture behavioural data — i.e. it is a phenomenological model (Simon 1969). M2 models not only the behaviour of the observed phenomena but also their context both in behavioural terms and situational terms. M2 becomes a description at the epistemological level rather than the implementational level. The crucial issue is not that M2 avoids all commitment to specifying internal structure, but firstly, that it is framed in appropriate categories (of objects and entities) to allow it to be created from observed data without prejudicing the available decisions with regard to implementation, and secondly, the cognitive burden in carrying out the abstraction process is minimized and supported. In the knowledge-engineering context this means that decisions relating to choice of knowledge representation language ('rules'), design decisions etc. are entered into only after the modelling language has been detailed and constructed and which then represents the totality of the expertise from an epistemological point of view. Within this description M3 and M4 are successively refined design models which become the blueprint for implementation (Hayward 1987).

2.3 CONTEXTUAL FRAMEWORKS FOR MODEL-DRIVEN KNOWLEDGE ENGINEERING

The model-driven activities previously described concentrate on what may be called the internal aspects of the system development process — the construction of the cognitive models of the observed behaviour. However, it is important that these models (M2, M3 and M4) and their construction are placed within some external framework. To this end, if we consider the development of a knowledge-based system as a process of production, then one is naturally led to the concept of the cycle of production (Hickman 1987). Conventional computing relates to the process of production in terms of the so-called software life-cycle model. Fig. 2.4 shows such a model.

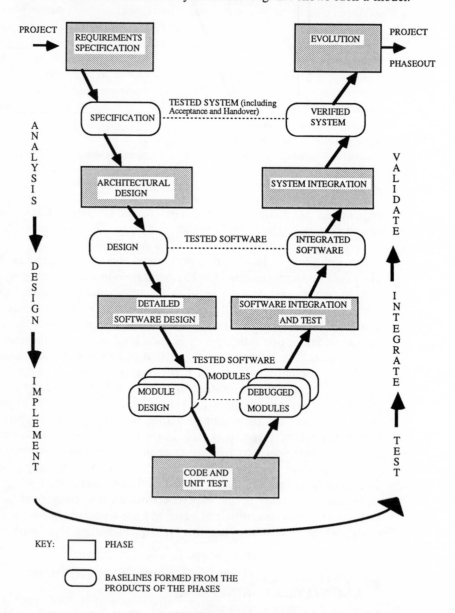

Fig. 2.4 — The Conventional Software Development Life-Cycle Model (STARTS 1987).

The view being presented here is that while the traditional view of AI programming and knowledge-based systems development might represent the 'craft'-based end of the production process, the model-driven approach lends itself to the life-cycle description which represents the 'mechanized' end of the production process. The power of this view lies in the fact that the life-cycle model itself becomes a model for project management and is a tool for project control. Each phase is defined in terms of the output produced during the phase, not by the activities occurring within the phase. A tangible output is the only criterion of progress — the only thing that the development team and management can assess objectively. To provide management control, the concept of baseline is introduced. The completion of a phase is determined by the satisfactory assessment of the quality of the defined products — the deliverables — of the phase; these deliverables then form the baseline for work in the next phase. However, this simplistic description of the life-cycle model and its representation in Fig. 2.4 are too rigorous and ignore real life constraints. In a real software development program it is very often the case that exploratory work on a subsequent phase, including costing, is usually required before a phase can be completed; that problems encountered in a later phase may involve reworking earlier phases; that users' requirements change; that incremental development may be used with different increments of the product in different phases of development; and that prototypes may be developed prior to the main development. In reality for large projects there are no clearly defined break-points between the various phases. Equally, any of the phases can be considered as a number of more or less sequential stages. This does not mean, however, that the life-cycle model description should be abandoned but rather that it represents a realistic portrayal of what is actually involved in the technical work of software development. Phases do indeed have to be imposed by project management; they will not happen of their own accord. To this end the definitions and concepts in the life-cycle model represent the best current understanding of software development methodology. It is for this reason that these ideas are carried over into knowledge-based systems development methodology. However, some very important caveats arise. In conventional software development the system specification results from a requirements analysis that can be described at three levels:

● Level 1   Introduction to the specification; background, outline systems requirement, outline system environment, structure of the document, definitions (lexicon) and references

● Level 2   User description; the environment, the users of the system, function, operation, life-cycle aspects, performance, constraints and assumptions

● Level 3   Functional specification; functional structure and interrelationships, data specifications and dictionary, overall system operational requirements and functional requirements

Constraints   Software design constraints, hardware design constraints and user design constraints
Life-cycle aspects; documentation, component testing and integrated testing, configuration and version
management, support services and maintenance
requirements and expansion requirements (evolution aspects)
Deliverables
Acceptance requirements
Project management (including quality assurance).

It is the viewpoint here that a knowledge-based system requirements analysis
should contain exactly the same levels of description, but in addition, an
internal requirement specification must be produced which defines those
non-procedural and procedural parts of the functional requirements that
model the expertise (STARTS 1987). To account for this the conventional
life-cycle model of Fig. 2.4 is amended to that of Fig. 2.5. Here full weight
is given to the model-driven approach.

From this point of view it can be seen that the creation of the conceptual
model (M2) is a phase in the overall life-cycle model and as such represents
an input into subsequent phases, notably the design phase. Here is not the
place for a full discussion of the issue of prototyping other than to emphasize
that in the model-driven approach prototyping is a goal-driven activity,
which might be invoked only to test certain aspects of the development
such as human–computer interface issues (menus, windows, mouse, etc.),
rather than a mini-model of the complete system.

2.4 THE CONCEPTUAL MODEL

A knowledge-based system is a model of some specific expertise built to
solve some specific problem. Like all modelling activities it involves the
refinement of a set of fuzzy data or information into some abstract structure.
The power of the modelling approach is that the model itself 'abstracts' and
'reveals' the underlying structure of the data/information — it in some way
explains the data or at least interprets it as a basis for explanation at a later
stage. This is indeed one of the major problems facing the knowledge
engineer when building a knowledge-based system — i.e. that of organizing
and understanding (Wielinga 1986).

The main purpose of a knowledge-based system is to solve problems. In
this case the data/information profile is a description of the problems and
their solution and the model should provide a mapping between them.
Although this viewpoint might indeed apply to conventional systems, the
fact that the problems solved by knowledge-based systems are generally
more complex than those which conventional systems attempt to solve
means that the model for expert problem solving should incorporate knowledge about the data/information and about its use. Therefore in this

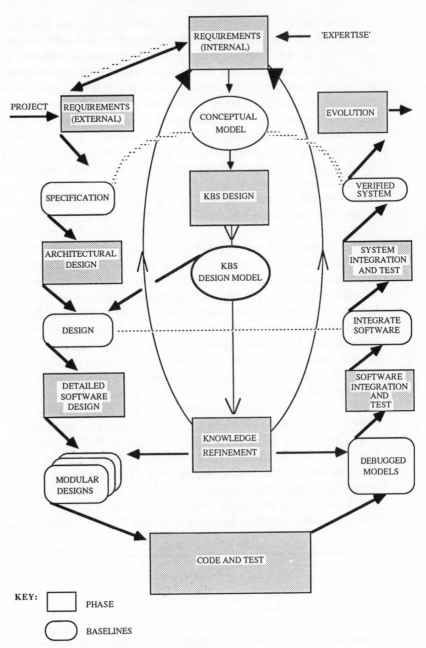

Fig. 2.5 — Knowledge-based Systems Development Life-cycle model.

purposefully complex domain (because we want to solve difficult problems) the model itself becomes not only a vehicle for description but also for interpretation — i.e. the knowledge engineer builds models into which he/she tries to fit the data as an aid to further analysis. The fact that this modelling activity has been made explicit here is new — in general the modelling process, if it occurs at all, is implicit in the systems-building process, which is unsatisfactory because it fails to make the model building and testing open to inspection and critique and does not allow the provision of support or constraint for the process. This failure is compounded and magnified when the development process is implementation oriented, i.e. the knowledge engineer thinks in terms of the data structures and procedures that might appear in the implemented system. While it is acknowledged that the mappings which the model provides between problems and solutions are necessarily more complicated in problems requiring expertise for their solution, the mappings between problems and solutions within the implementation-oriented framework of data structures and procedures are even more difficult. In the language of Fig. 2.3 the mappings are trying to incorporate the transformations from M2 to M4 rather than within M2 itself.

The purpose of the conceptual model is to provide a modelling language that will represent the problem-solving activities at a reasonably high level of abstraction and generality. To this end it is possible to construct models which describe the prototypical character of classes of problem-solving behaviour — we call them interpretation models. The knowledge engineer then uses these interpretation models as a starting point for knowledge analysis and the knowledge-engineering process becomes one of model refinement rather than one of model creation. From the wider perspective this will enable a wider audience to benefit from the methodology as in conventional development methodologies. However, until a comprehensive library of interpretation models is provided, model construction will continue to be a task of the knowledge engineer following this methodology.

The modelling language developed in Esprit Project 1098 incorporates four layers of description, each containing different types of knowledge which incorporates the static (factual) and dynamic (strategic) nature of the knowledge which underlies expertise. Thus we have strategic knowledge which controls the task knowledge which applies the inferential knowledge which itself describes the domain knowledge. Fig. 2.6 illustrates these ideas.

Level	Relation	Objects	Organisation
domain level	describes	concepts, relations and structures	axiomatic structures
inference level	applies	meta–classes, knowledge sources	inference structures
task level	controls	goals, tasks	task structure
strategic level		plans, meta–rules, repairs, impasses	process structure

Fig. 2.6 — Layers of Description of Expert Knowledge (Wielinga 1986).

The first layer contains the so-called static knowledge of the domain: domain concepts, relations and complex structures, such as models of processes or devices. In a marketing context we might include here concepts such as price, product, share, mix, niche, etc. or relations such as price/ volume ratio. The system model prevalent in this domain could be as loose as 'everything is price, product, place, promotion' or it might be some more formalized marketing model. The problem in marketing is that there exist very few if any axiomatic structures. This is why the marketing process has been assumed to be too complex for conventional computer analysis. The second layer is the inference layer. In this layer we describe what inferences can be made on the knowledge in the domain layer. Two types of entities (knowledge categories) are represented within the inference layer: meta-classes and knowledge sources. Meta-classes describe the role that domain concepts can play in a reasoning process. Therefore, following the same example, we might have the domain object or concept of price playing the role of constraint in the inferencing processes guiding marketing strategy — it might also play the role of result in some other aspect of the planning process. Knowledge sources describe what types of inferences can be made on the basis of the relations in the domain layer. Therefore we might have the knowledge source *compare* which will link domain concept *price* with domain concept *cost* or sales. The inference and the domain layers combine to form what is best considered as a 'theory' of the domain. They define what can be known and what can be inferred but say nothing about how such knowledge is actually applied to reason towards some desired conclusion(s).

The third layer is the task layer which now begins to define how the knowledge expressed in the two previous layers is used in a problem-solving context. At this level the basic objects are goals and tasks related as in Fig. 2.7.

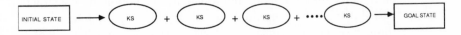

Fig. 2.7 — Task decomposition in terms of knowledge sources.

Tasks are ways in which knowledge sources (things which relate objects/ relations, etc. of the domain) are combined to achieve a particular goal. The fourth layer is the strategic layer in which meta-knowledge resides, namely that knowledge which allows a system to make plans — i.e. create a task structure — control and monitor the execution of tasks, diagnose when something goes wrong and possibly find repairs for impasses. Very often the strategic layer represents those rules of thumb (heuristics) in common use within a particular domain. In marketing, for example, a common strategic layer meta-rule is 'if you cannot specify a strategy that meets the objectives then change the objectives'.

It is important to realize that there is no real theoretical justification for this taxonomy other than expedience. The syntactic differentiation represented by the four layers does however have an intuitively satisfying semantic level of description and has been demonstrated repeatedly to have been of a high degree of pragmatic utility. The conceptual model is a major output of the analysis phase and combines with the external requirements to form the system specification. By its very nature it is domain-dependent and therefore of limited re-usability.

Good methodologies usually incorporate aspects or components that are actually re-usable i.e. transferable. While the idea and structure of the conceptual model are transferable, the model itself is not — because of its domain dependence. It is a natural step to abstract one further degree and obtain a domain-independent model.

2.5 THE INTERPRETATION MODEL

Although it has to be acknowledged that expertise comes in many varieties, it is a major assumption (supported by experience) that at some level of abstraction, expertise — i.e. human problem solving — can be classified. Domains may contain different concepts but they may also share common knowledge and common strategies. In particular, it seems possible that inference mechanisms that are domain-independent may be identified. Psychometric research (Guilford 1967, Sternberg 1982), modelling of human problem-solving research and knowledge-engineering research (Clancey 1985, Chandrasekaran 1983, Hayes-Roth et al. 1983) seem to support this view. Thus a conceptual model can be abstracted from its domain-specific content and function to become some sort of skeletal model of expertise in another domain performing a relatively similar task. Such an abstracted model is called an interpretation model. The role of the interpretation model is a template structure that allows for some top-down refinement from verbal data rather than the more ambitious task of bottom-up construction from verbal data to the conceptual model. In this way the interpretation model through selection becomes an intermediary between 'what to look for in the verbal data' and the conceptual model that is to be constructed. Here the concept of re-usability manifests itself with precise clarity. To this end the conceptual model is a product of the knowledge-engineering process while the interpretation model is a tool. Interpretation models themselves can be further abstracted into generic models which represent so-called 'pure tasks', i.e. elementary problem-solving tasks. Such tasks can stand on their own if problem input is well-defined and produces a solution. This solution may well be used in other tasks but it is the 'answer' to some original (pure) problem. However, because real life expertise normally includes a combi-nation of various elementary tasks — the generic or pure tasks — we also identify the real life models. Real life models are composites of generic models. Although they are abstracted from a specific domain, there may still be some higher-level domain dependencies left in the model, which may constrain the scope of the applicability of real life models. Real life models may assume certain similar structures across domains or even similarities in the functionality of the expertise that has led to a particular composition of tasks. The construction/refinement procedure is shown in Fig. 2.8. Generic models are thus the essential ingredients in the use of

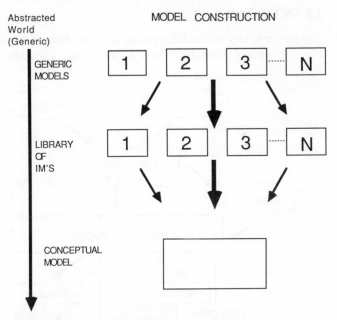

Fig. 2.8 — Model construction and refinement.

interpretation models. It is assumed that the number of generic tasks — or of prototypical generic tasks — is a manageable though large set. The set is described, incompletely, by the taxonomy in Fig. 2.9.

In refining/constructing the final conceptual model the knowledge

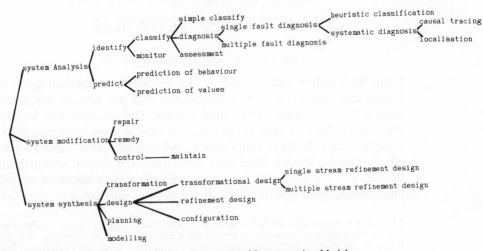

Fig. 2.9 — Taxonomy of Interpretation Models.

engineer may either have a suitable real life model available to use as an interpretation model or, as is more likely, will have to construct one from the available generic models.

2.6 AN EXAMPLE

The power in any methodology must lie in the re-usability of its components. Fig. 2.10 shows this aspect for a major project currently under way at the

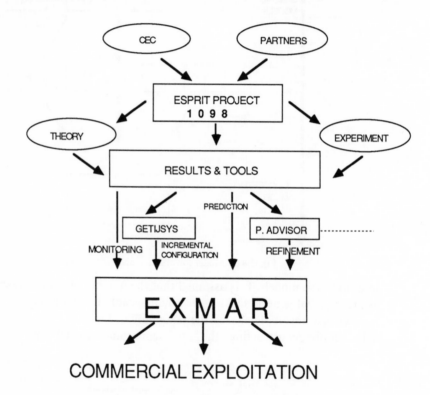

Fig. 2.10 — Reusable components in Exmar.

South Bank Polytechnic. Exmar† — Expert System in Marketing — is a project that aims to build an expert system that will provide the decision support for the marketing-planning process. This example will hopefully show how to build in context the use of models as re-usable components of a methodology. Getijsys and Pensions Advisor are other projects within which re-usable models have been developed, and re-used within Exmar (Killin 1987, Mulhall 1987). Inputs to the Exmar project consist of, amongst other things, those generic models that can be reconstructed to provide the

---

† Exmar is a project with the South Bank Polytechnic and Langton Ltd as Co-Developers. The DTI is a major sponsor and at present the Exmar Club has ten members: ICI, Rolls-Royce, Wight, Collins, Rutherford, Scott, Simon Engineering, Wellcome Foundation, British Airways, Royal Mail (Parcels), British Telecom, NCR and Compaq.

basis for the construction of the conceptual model that will be the Exmar system.

The framework for the marketing-planning process has been provided by Professor McDonald of Cranfield (McDonald 1987). Fig. 2.11 shows this

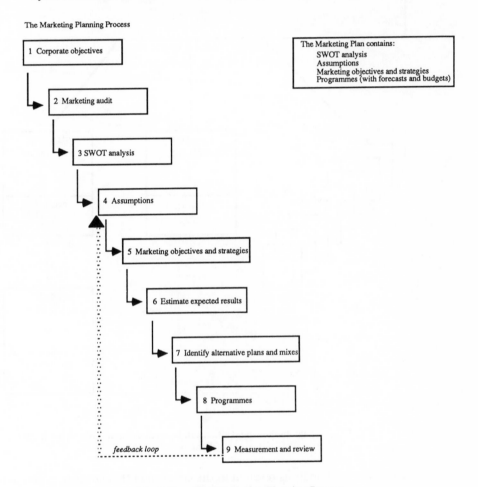

Fig. 2.11 — The Marketing Planning Process.

framework. Initial interviews with marketing experts intimated that a feasible framework for Exmar itself might well be as a monitor to the planning process, since it was very quickly established that a KBS solution to the process of producing a marketing plan was a huge task — although possible — which could not be tackled within budget limits. A preliminary proposal for the system was a task decomposition as illustrated in Fig. 2.12.

Within this task structure was the identification of a strategy evaluation subtask. Interestingly, the external requirements analysis that has been mentioned earlier highlighted the importance of the strategy evaluation component in the planning process itself and it is therefore not unexpected that it should manifest itself within the monitoring task. Further knowledge

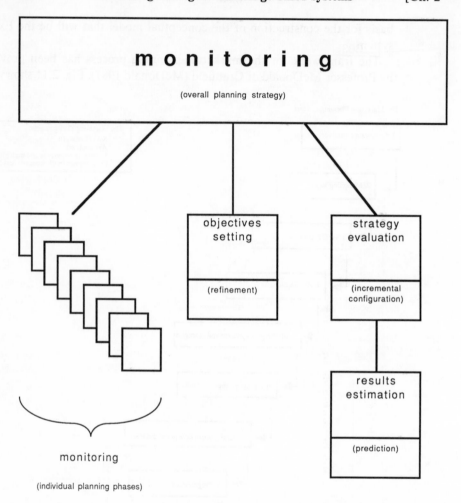

Fig. 2.12 — Diagram showing relationship between different tasks in the Exmar domain.

elicitation and analysis resulted in the conclusion that strategy evaluation is a form of incremental configuration. The inference structure for incremental configuration had previously been constructed in a very distinct domain–tidal wave analysis — within the Getijsys project shown in Fig. 2.10. This inference structure is shown in Fig. 2.13.

In order to understand this configuration model it is best to use an everyday example. We will go on to show its instantiation within the marketing-planning domain. Take the example of configuring a human face, as in say design, from the universe of all 'observables' relating to facial features. (The potato-man problem!). Here one sees how the inference mechanism combines meta-classes (sets of ears, eyes, noses, etc. at various stages of the process) to arrive at the stated task of constructing a pretty female face. Subjective elements make up the termination criteria — we

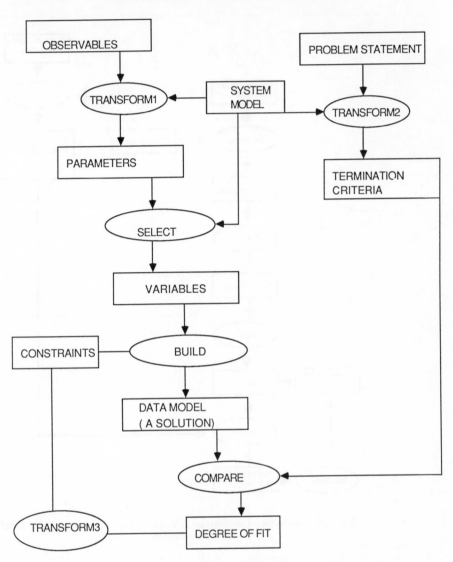

Fig. 2.13 — Inference Structure — Incremental Configuration.

would all accept that a pretty female face must have two eyes, two ears, etc. arranged in a particular way; we might however disagree as to the size, colour, etc.

This example will now help us to understand the instantiated model for strategy evaluation within the marketing-planning process and consequently the role these models play in the development methodology. Here it is important to note that it is justified to modify the generic model in that the system model is well-known and universally agreed to be that which governs price, place, product and promotion and therefore may be omitted.

The inference structure is only one aspect of the interpretation model as

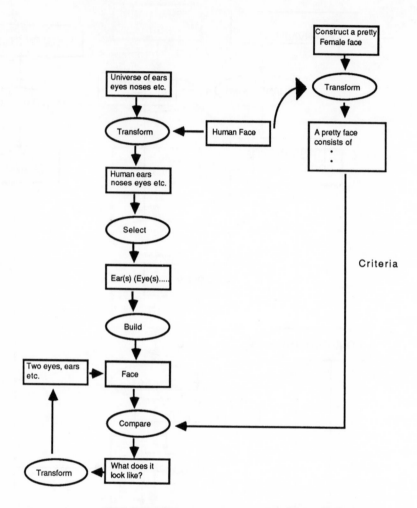

Fig. 2.14 — Instantiated incremental configuration inference structure for facial construction.

can be seen from Fig. 2.15. However, it represents one of the parts which is most useful for the interpretation of the protocols derived from the verbal data obtained from the expert — hence the name for the models. The process of model construction then becomes one of initial selection, possible rejection, refinement and modification. The details of the model are 'fleshed out' from the analysis of the verbal data. We have found this model-driven approach to be both fruitful in its suggestiveness and, more importantly for commercial applications, pragmatic. The full-blown conceptual model together with the external requirements will combine to form the knowledge-based system specification, which would be a major deliverable within the life-cycle.

The conclusion of the analysis phase (Figs 2.4 and 2.5) with the KBS specification as the main deliverable leads directly and naturally into design.

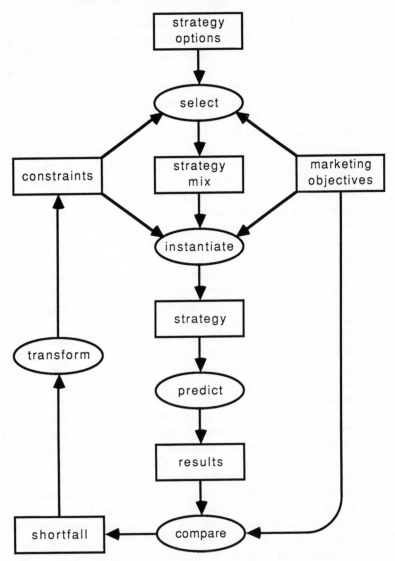

Fig. 2.15 — Inference structure for strategy formulation/evaluation.

2.7 DESIGN FRAMEWORK FOR KBS DEVELOPMENT

Within KBS development there is no well-defined process or language for design. We must of course follow conventional 'good' design procedures but take account of the special nature of KBS. This special nature manifests itself in choosing those methods, mainly AI methods, that enable identified and by now specified functionalities that represent 'expertise' to be implemented. For the purposes of this chapter we will be looking only at architectural design rather than detailed software design. In terms of Fig. 2.3 we are discussing only model M3 rather than M4, M5, etc. Within the development life-cycle the architectural design phase represents a key transition point in that it is the point at which a set of requirements is turned into a perception of how the system may achieve its goals. To this end, this phase aims at producing a verified specification of the overall hardware and software architecture, data structure, AI methods, components and interfaces for the software product, along with peripheral components relating to user manuals and testing.

The specification, which is a compilation of the external and internal analyses, combines to produce of set of functional and non-functional requirements. The KBS life-cycle model of Fig. 2.5 suggests that functional requirements specific to the knowledge-based component of the system may, ideally, be developed in parallel with the externally based functionalities. Theoretically this should be possible, although such is our knowledge at present that this is seldom the case and there is little understood interplay between the two activities.

The design process is highly creative and therefore it is not possible to give a prescriptive recipe for the KBS design process. However, one advantage with the model-driven approach is that within the conceptual model itself there can appear some clear guidelines for the design process, both in terms of functional specification and identification of design components (including AI methods), which enable the subsequent detailed design phase to proceed. The importance of the four-layer conceptual model lay in the fact that often it enables a straightforward transformation from the components that make up the conceptual model into those components that make up the design model. The initial design process consists of a functional description which is then rapidly transformed into identifying individual components or groups of components which, working together, support each required function (both internal and external). These components will then be composed into a set of modular designs as described in Fig. 2.5. This process is described in Fig. 2.16. Here we include conventional design paradigms — e.g. Yourden and Constantine — and AI paradigms. The latter, however, is at present sadly lacking in a definitive description of applicability — i.e. there is no definitive list of AI paradigms which relate automatically or sensibly to the knowledge components of the analysis model. This is why KBS design is difficult and a state-of-the-art activity.

However, an example of the power of the four-layer model is shown in Fig. 2.17. This represents a simplified transformation in that it is possible to identify on a one-to-one basis analysis model components with design model components. When complex methods, AI or otherwise, are involved, a more complex type of transformation which cuts vertically through the layers to map to the corresponding design component might be necessary. The importance of the approach is that the four-layer model usually gives clear indication, i.e. a basic framework to enable this transformation.

From the point of view of a complete description of the design phase, the preceding description is less than adequate. However, it is possible to list the end-products of the architectural design phase which incorporate both KBS and conventional wisdom. Remember that it is the thesis of this chapter that these are not mutually incompatible. These products are as follows:

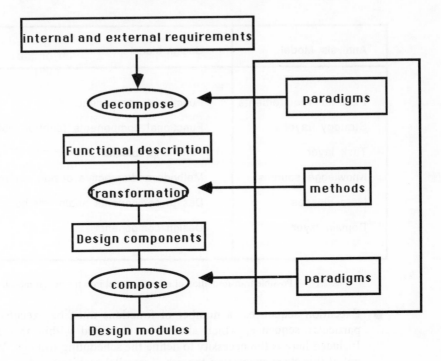

Fig. 2.16 — KBS design framework.

● Functional components; the design process should provide a description of all the functions contained in the functional requirement (of the requirements specification). A traceability analysis should be possible that identifies which design components or combination of components work together to support each and every identified and required function. It is here especially that prototyping may be used.

● Performance criteria; this is an aspect of KBS development which is usually totally ignored — a reason why so many implementations have led to disappointment. The requirements analysis should have laid down guidelines for the performance parameters. However, it is not until the methods have been selected or created that it is possible to establish that these criteria have been met, fully or partially. An overlay to the design process described above is the need to take account of traffic patterns and data volumes previously identified in the requirements analysis. It is at this stage that items of information such as hardware transfer times (i.e. disc transfers) should be taken into account. Complex and time-consuming AI methods should be analysed at this stage for performance and a quid pro quo arrangement established against functionality. This is a design decision not to be left to the implementation stage.

● Simultaneous access of data/knowledge; the design stage must clearly indicate where knowledge or data sources are to be simultaneously accessible. The overall aim is to ensure integrity.

Analysis Model	Design Model
External requirements	Functional components
Strategy layer	Functional components (control methods)
Task layer	Functional blocks
Knowledge sources	Methods and/or active design components
Meta–classes	Design components and/or methods
Domain layer	Design components

Fig. 2.17 — Possible transformation of analysis model into the design model.

● Execution sequences; a number of functions must be executed in a particular sequence, which should be identified within this phase. Included here is the necessity to define the scheduling strategy. We are not at this stage suggesting the use of parallel architectures.
● Human–computer/human factor issues; the principles upon which these extremely important decisions are based should be addressed here.
● Hardware configuration; in KBS development this might be one of the most contentious issues — the mapping of the design components to the target hardware. Very often many of the preceding discussions are collapsed into the hardware choice — shell, package, environment — which should only be undertaken after analysis and design have been rigorously explored. The failure to adopt this procedure is why so many unused and incomplete shell systems are left on the shelf or expensive hardware/environment configurations are left gathering dust!
● Testing; again a much ignored area in KBS development, but one which is important. The design documentation should define how the derived design model can support an adequate testing strategy.
● Database interface; if the KBS development includes access to and integration with a substantial on-line database, then attention must be given, in the conventional sense, to logical data (knowledge structure). The design must highlight these parameters, including the logical to physical mappings that have been assumed, perhaps at the analysis stage.

2.8 CONCLUSIONS

The model-driven approach expounded in this chapter is not the definitive solution to the problems of KBS development. The approach does however enable the identification of a methodical approach, i.e. a methodology, and also lends guidance to the passage through the life-cycle of the development process. There is much to be done and many inconsistencies and flaws in the procedures to be reconciled. However, at present we believe that this approach affords the best accommodation of conventional wisdom. More strongly, we believe that KBS developments are not fundamentally different from conventional systems development, merely more complex. To this end, those constraints and procedural approaches that software engineering endeavours to impose on ordinary systems development should be readily transportable to KBS development. If nothing else, this chapter should indicate that this approach is viable and desirable.

ACKNOWLEDGEMENT

Much of this work has been supported in part by the Esprit program of the Commission of the European Community under contract P1098. Partners in the project are STL, SCICON, SCS, Cap Sogeti and University of Amsterdam.

REFERENCES

Chandrasekaran, B. (1983) Towards a taxonomy for problem solving. *AI Magazine* **4** 9–18

Clancey, W. J. (1985) Heuristic classification. *Artificial Intelligence* **27** 215–251

Guilford, J. P. (1967) *The nature of human intelligence*. Academic Press, New York

Hayes-Roth, F., Waterman, D. A., & Lenat, D. B. (1983) *Building expert systems*. Addison-Wesley, Reading, MA

Hayward, S. (1987) The KADS Methodology: Analysis and Design for Knowledge Based Systems. Report Y1. Esprit Project 1098

Hickman, F. R. (1987) The Role of Requirement Analysis in KBS Development. KBSC publications

Killin, J. L. (1987) The Getijsys Expert System Project. Qualitative reasoning module: Model document. KBSC publications

McDonald, M. H. B. (1987) *Marketing plans*. Heinemann, London

Mulhall, T. (1987) Monitoring Tasks in Marketing Planning. Exmar Project. KBSC publications

Simon, H. A. (1969) *The sciences of the artificial*. MIT Press, Cambridge Ma

Sternberg, R. J. (ed.) (1982) *Handbook of human intelligence*. Cambridge University Press, Cambridge

STARTS (1987) *The STARTS guide*. 2nd ed., vol. 1. NCC publications

Wielinga, B. J. (1986) Models of expertise. *Proceedings of ECAI 1986*

3

Knowledge elicitation: Principles and practice

Mike Greenwell

3.1 INTRODUCTION

What is knowledge engineering about? Are there any tried and tested techniques of obtaining and representing knowledge as a working computer system? Moving up from knowledge elicitation techniques, what do we know of the methodologies behind the building of expert systems? Do any exist? Are they useful? In order to try to answer these questions, this chapter explores the relationship between knowledge engineering and psychology in the form of a fairly broad review of recent writings on knowledge engineering (mostly written by psychologists) with a strong emphasis on knowledge elicitation but also including other related issues in knowledge engineering.

Psychology is difficult to define adequately, being largely an umbrella term. It is concerned with behaviour — either individual, group or animal behaviour — while cognitive psychology is concerned with the processes by which thinking is possible. Psychology also deals with creativity, a concept which is even more difficult to define than psychology itself; personality, that unknown quantity which accounts for individual differences, and developmental processes including the ability to learn. It is not too important what psychology is. What is important is what psychologists do with respect to knowledge engineering. In this chapter that will mostly be concerned with knowledge elicitation issues.

3.2 PROBLEMS WITH PROBLEM SOLVING

The first contribution of psychology to knowledge engineering is the study of human thinking, and problem solving in particular. Human reasoning is far from perfect. Studies have demonstrated that people have difficulty in estimating probabilities (Tversky & Kahnemann 1974), that the operation of logic seemingly plays no part in our reasoning, even when attempting to solve syllogisms (Johnson-Laird 1983) and that information which includes disjunctive information is more difficult for people to accept than conjunctive information (Bruner et al. 1956)

Many people have great problems dealing with assigning probability to alternative outcomes. Evidence suggests that most people cannot (Spetzler & Stael Von Holstein 1975, Kidd & Cooper 1983) and when values are given they are unreliable, differing on separate occasions and, strangely enough, even on the time of day (Doyle 1983). When asked to estimate positive and negative weights in a two-by-two frequency table the tendency is for people to overestimate the positive weights (Shweder 1977). Negative information is rarely used by subjects when solving syllogisms (Wason & Johnson-Laird 1972).

Errors in problem solving come about through such processes as illusory correlation, gambler's fallacy and regression bias. Cleaves (1988) takes on the unenviable task of attempting to detect deficiencies in expert problem solving on the assumption that expert thinking is, after all, human thinking, and human thinking can be improved upon. In this role the knowledge engineer is called upon to understand the domain and the expert's problem-solving behaviour, and then to identify and correct any cognitive biases.

Knowledge engineering as a solution to erroneous problem solving is rather 'jumping the gun'. The first point of issue is how knowledge engineering is possible at all. Knowledge engineering is a specialized form of the computer modelling of cognitive processes or intelligent behaviour. Computer modelling itself began with the logic theorem provers of Newell *et al.* in 1957 and GPS, the General Problem Solver of Newell & Simon, in 1961. The explicit link between psychological processes and computer processing was made by Miller *et al.* in 1960, producing a new branch of psychology — computational psychology. Computational psychologists are identified by three ways of theorizing (Boden 1988). Firstly, they take a functionalist approach to mental phenomena which is suitable to computer science's dependence upon effective procedures. Secondly, for the computer psychologist the mind is conceived as a representational system — i.e. mental procedures are characterized as computational processes which construct mental representations. Lastly, and as an aside, neuro-science, the working of the brain, is conceived as a computational system such as a multi-tasking parallel processor. This is becoming more important with the increasing availability of parallel-processing computers.

The critics of the GPS thought that the psychological processes as identified by Newell & Simon were unlike those of the human mind and more properly belonged to computers. This led them to assert that Newell & Simon's approach was largely irrelevant to psychology. Even if this is the case, it does not invalidate their important, although historical, contribution to artificial intelligence and knowledge engineering. The success of their simulations of mental phenomena cannot be divorced from a system performance point of view (Newell & Simon 1972, Card *et al.* 1983). Although GPS was quite limited when it came to simulating human thinking, the problems it solved had to have a very simple cognitive structure whilst the problems themselves had to be simplistic, largely owing to computational constraints. Where GPS really failed was in the assumption that all problems could be solved by searching through representations of different states until a solution could be found.

Early computer modelling, irrespective of purported successes or failures, is the predecessor of demonstratively successful knowledge engineering. The early work on computer modelling demonstrated that modelling intelligent processes was possible, the main thrust of the research being how this could best be done and how to obtain and represent highly complex and esoteric domain knowledge.

3.3 PROBLEMS WITH KNOWLEDGE ELICITATION

Knowledge elicitation is the process of extracting domain expertise, which includes facts, explanations, justifications, rules of thumb and procedures given by a recognized domain expert. Efficient knowledge engineering requires answering some fundamental questions in psychology (Kidd 1987). An example of psychological issues which impinge upon knowledge elicitation is the relationship between knowledge and language, and an adequate theory of human problem solving.

Although neurology, psychology, linguistics, education, sociology, philosophy and systems theories are relevant to knowledge engineering, there is little likely gain from a detailed investigation of what these relationships actually are (Gaines 1988).

One line of research is directed towards improving elicitation techniques, and expanding the number of techniques if necessary. Studies concentrating upon the effectiveness of the methods used by knowledge engineers are rare. The required information is how effective each method is and in what situation. Although there are some useful commentaries on knowledge acquisition methods, there are few objective results to guide the designers in the selection of knowledge acquisition techniques, the anticipation of problems or the estimation of progress (Fox *et al.* 1987).

It must be noted that knowledge is not transferred by any interactive technique. Knowledge is a mental state which implies something is understood and that understanding has a cognitive representation fixed, at least temporarily, in the beholder's mind. All any technique can do is assist the development of the understanding by an efficient transfer of data. The most common form of data is by utterance, but other forms include text, diagrams, tables or video.

Gammack (1987) evaluates techniques suitable for discovering the conceptual organization of domain knowledge. A worthy endeavour is not assisted by the use of a non-expert as correspondent (e.g. a scientist with an interest in the domain). We are left wondering whether or not a practising expert would make a different organization of their knowledge. There have been numerous studies which have demonstrated the differences between novices and experts. There is none, that I am aware of, that compares interested amateurs with experts.

Gammack looks at a number of techniques borrowed from traditional psychology designed to reveal the conceptual and structural organization of domain knowledge. Concept elicitation consists of asking the informant to prepare a talk outlining the whole domain. This forms the basis of a tutorial interview. Structure elicitation includes the card-sort method, multi-dimensional scaling and the repertory grid technique. The card-sort uses cards which represent specific or canonical objects in the domain. The expert sorts the cards and with relevant explanations assists the knowledge engineer in perceiving the category structure for the domain of expertise.

Gammack concludes that the tutorial interview is good for an orientation to the domain, providing a lot of relevant material, and is relatively undemanding on the expert. However, the coverage is incomplete and somewhat arbitrary and requires a good level of interview skills. The result of using a card-sort is a cluster of concepts, relationships and various structures (e.g. hierarchical). Card-sort is easy to perform and is useful for segmenting the domain into manageable areas. Multi-dimensional scaling provides a global picture of the similarity of domain concepts, and dimensions for distinguishing objects. The technique does not require the presence of the knowledge engineer, whose only function is to design the questionnaire and interpret the results: even statistical analysis can be delegated to a computer. (The results of such an analysis, however, can be indecipherable and may have little use.) Proximity analysis is a complement to multi-dimensional scaling, the result of which is a network representation of domain concepts demonstrating meaningful links between concepts and objects.

The repertory grid, Gammack reports, is good for capturing the fine detail in the distinctions between concepts and has the advantage of working at the level of the expert's personal constructs. This is exceptionally beneficial when there is no public vocabulary and few constraints on the range of domain concepts. However, interpreting the resulting knowledge may lead to problems of validation. Gammack reports that the repertory grid is very time-consuming, a finding with major commercial implications and one which contrasts with the views of Shaw & Gaines (1987).

The lack of an accredited expert in Gammack's assessment of techniques should not distract from the confirmation that a particular technique is capable of eliciting the required knowledge. The study, however, leaves a number of questions unanswered. More research is needed as to how techniques are integrated and where they would fit into an actual project. It is also unclear what form the data takes and whether a knowledge engineer would feel confident in implementing the knowledge analysis elicited from the techniques. Obtaining the data is part of the process. Using the data as the basis of a knowledge base is proof of the technique as other researchers have noted (Fox et al. 1987).

Schweickert et al. (1988) carry out a study which attempts to perform a psychological experiment with knowledge elicitation as the subject matter. Three knowledge elicitation methods are subjected to various tests of effectiveness. The techniques studied were structured interview, 20 questions and card-sort, and the domain of expertise was industrial lighting.

The structured interview (Breuker & Wielinga 1984) is characterized by the desire of the knowledge engineer to elicit fairly specific information in some depth and assumes that the knowledge engineer has already gained a more than cursory appreciation of the domain through focused interviews (see Greenwell 1988). The 20 questions technique is based on an old radio guessing game; and is characterized by allowing only 'yes' or 'no' answers.

The metrics of success by which the three methods are compared are the number of rules which were derived from the specific method, the degree of agreement between knowledge engineers as to the validity of the rules and the number of rules which could be implemented in the expert system. It is interesting to note that the same method used in both Gammack's and Schweickert et al.'s study resulted in entirely different data. The card-sort is capable of producing rules and structures. Quite obviously it is not only the method which is important but the intention underlining its use.

The major criticism of Schweickert et al. (1988) is the degree of realism which the case study has in comparison to an actual (commercial) expert system project. In describing this work as a case study it is assumed that it is a systematic observation of some aspect of the world as it exists, and not confined within an artificial laboratory environment.

What Schweickert et al. seem to have is a laboratory experiment which is contrived to look like a case study. This leads to the important question: does the unreality of the study affect the conclusions? Although it does not necessarily follow that a contrived study will produce contrived results, the conclusions must be suspect.

What then would a real case study look like? The suggestion is that findings which are intended to apply to commercial knowledge engineering must be derived from a commercial context. Projects must be real projects and experts mu . be real experts. This would be far more difficult for the researchers to come to terms with since the first priority of a knowledge engineer is to achieve project targets, not advance the limits of human knowledge. The researcher must take one of two roles in a realistic case study, either participatory or non-participatory. Participating in the project as a knowledge engineer gives the researcher direct insight into the problems, frustrations and elations of the knowledge engineer; but objectivity is lost. A non-participatory role with frequent debriefing sessions of the knowledge engineer and expert coupled with suitable analysis will give a more objective overview of the knowledge elicitation processes.

It is likely that the researcher involved in a commercial project would appreciate that there is more to a knowledge elicitation technique than the number of rules derived, the extent of agreement and the number of rules implemented. Knowledge implementation is a by-product of the process of learning and understanding the expert's domain and method. There will be times when, according to Schweickert et al.'s criteria, nothing is achieved (i.e. no rules generated for negotiation or implementation) but the knowledge engineer will be quite happy with the progress made just by coming to terms with a complex problem.

So what can be made of Schweickert et al.'s conclusions that the twenty questions technique led to more rules than the card-sort, but that the twenty questions technique was responsible for the lowest percentage of rules agreed to with the expert? Taking into account a point raised by Schweickert *et al.*, that the order of the techniques may have a significant effect on the project, perhaps it would appear that the results are of little consequence. The ordering of the techniques is a vital issue since it influences the states of knowledge of the participants, and in this respect perhaps only traditional psychological research can reveal the effects of the order of techniques. Perhaps it is easier to assume that such knowledge is of little value after all, and then use our discretion and common sense based on experience instead.

Fox *et al.* (1987) have researched the role and application of expert systems in the domain of medical diagnosis for many years, and using leukemia diagnosis as the domain for a case study would seem a sensible choice. However, the choice of a domain, even one in the general area of many years of research, is not a trivial matter. At first, Fox *et al.* thought the choice of domain to be too small and insufficiently complex. However, the domain proved to be more complicated than the researchers expected.

The specific domain characteristics must be a major determinant in a research project. Too simple a domain provides no real test at all, while a domain which is too complex requires more work than was initially anticipated, with less being completed, and intellectual resources earmarked for discovering the effectiveness of knowledge acquisition methods are used for understanding the domain knowledge. Furthermore, a complex application will not have uniform progress, since identification of those areas of the application where acceptable performances provide the knowledge engineers with a greater challenge is problematic. The success or failure of a specific knowledge-engineering technique is determined by the contribution of the technique to the performance of a system as judged by the expert. Fox *et al.* conclude that statements about rapid or slow progress in knowledge acquisition are meaningless in isolation. A true assessment is the performance of the system. It is interesting that the conclusions of the research are more in the realm of guidelines for project management; the aim of the research, however, was to test knowledge acquisition techniques. Fox *et al.* provide little hard information as to what techniques are good and when, but this is not unexpected since they had a realistic domain, expert and project. What they found was that it is not easy to assess techniques.

So far the studies have dealt with the assessment of techniques with single experts. However, some projects necessitate more than one expert. Multi-expert projects are necessary either because the proposed system requires input from more than one person or because numerous experts are available, and input from a selection is an organizational plus. McGraw & Seale (1988) investigate group-orientated methods for dealing with multiple experts. It has long been known that small-group judgement tends to be better than individual judgement (Eisenson *et al.* 1963). A major advantage of group judgement over individual judgement described by Shaw (1932), is that while the group may not identify the optimum solution they have the ability to recognize and reject incorrect solutions. The group comes into its own when the problem can be divided into parts which utilize the specialized talents of specific group members (Steiner 1972). Slater (1958) suggested that the optimum size of a group should be 'five', whilst McGraw & Seale (1988) prefer 'three', although 'three' is a very small group indeed.

The knowledge elicitation methods suggested by McGraw & Seale follow an initial session of brainstorming. This well-known technique is ascribed to Osborn (1953) who was concerned that organizations were failing to produce original business ideas. The reason seemed largely due to the unwillingness of lower-ranked personnel to contradict their superiors. McGraw & Seale suggest the use of brainstorming in knowledge-engineering projects with a number of experts helping experts and the knowledge engineers breaking away from conventional solutions. This appears to run counter to common sense since there is no good reason why non-conventional thinking should be encouraged in the initial interviews. Much later in the project non-conventional thinking may have some benefits, but this is arguable. The benefit of brainstorming is a wider coverage of the subject matter but at the cost of an almost total lack of structure. A secondary benefit is the chance it affords everyone to have a say since none of the contributions are evaluated until later.

The second technique suggested by McGraw & Seale, which can either follow brainstorming or be used independently, is consensus decision making, originally documented by Cragan & Wright (1980). The goal of this technique is to discover the best solution to a problem by assessing the strengths and weaknesses of possible solutions. Each expert provides their own opinion and the optimum solution is reached by voting on the alternatives.

The third group technique — the nominal group technique (Huseman 1973) — is an attempt to counter the effect of status differences between the experts which may distort communication. In this technique the advantages and disadvantages of the set of possible solutions are listed without discussion. After the knowledge engineer has amalgamated and represented the lists, each expert anonymously ranks the advantages and disadvantages. This is followed by a discussion of the rankings with the aim of choosing the optimum solution.

The final technique reviewed by McGraw & Seale is debriefing, by which they simply mean bringing the session to an end. A major benefit from the debriefing session is the degree of confidence or certainty of each expert in the derived knowledge or optimum solution. Debriefing may be a group process or held on an individual basis. McGraw & Seale suggest techniques which are suitable for multiple-expert projects but they do not evaluate them in any systematic way, the basic principle being that because these techniques worked for them in unspecified projects then they deserve consideration. McGraw & Seale's basic assumption is that if the project requires more than one expert then group techniques are more favourable. This cannot be accepted on faith. They may well be right in their assertion, but groups of experts can only mean increased development costs and many people will need to be persuaded that this extra cost is justified.

Even with multiple-expert projects all or part of the whole task is performed by a single person. What is obviously wanted is a detailed commentary of the performance either as it happens or shortly afterwards. This technique of obtaining the expert's own detailed account is known as 'self-report', 'introspection' or 'talk-aloud protocols'. Reports fall into one of four basic categories depending upon whether the report is a primary or secondary task together with a temporal dimension of whether the report is given concurrently or retrospectively. A primary task refers to introspection pure and simple. A secondary task is when the expert concentrates upon the task and gives the report as an aside. The reporting does not interfere with the performance of the task. Another variation would be to report on critical events. Bainbridge (1979) confirmed that people are more likely to recognize operational principles than recall them. People are also more likely to recall critical or outstanding events. The critical incident technique was first described by Flanagan (1954) and very largely consists of discussing the experiences of memorable events.

3.4 PROBLEMS OF SPEAKING WHILE THINKING

There is a long history of psychological research using think-aloud data. The technique came into disrepute more often because it did not fit with current models of mind or psychological paradigms than because of genuine criticisms of the technique. In an early criticism Buhler (1908) rejected self-report because of the implication that thinking was possible without the use of images — this was in contradiction to his current theories. A more severe blow to introspective methods was brought about by the rise and dominance of behaviourism. Introspection became a secondary and largely European technique. It was used to great effect by Piaget while investigating the cognitive processes of children. In its early appliance to knowledge engineering, Kassirer & Gorry (1978) found that introspection was useful in producing rules but not for the higher-level strategies by which they were applied.

There are many problems with self-report but the most significant one is the huge amount of time it takes to get some results. Kleinmuntz (1968) collected 60 hours of audio tape and achieved 26 rules in one domain, but in a more complex domain 192 hours led to very little useful information. This problem could be overcome by holding back the use of self-report to a later stage in the project when the knowledge engineer has enough knowledge of the domain to guide and structure the elicitation sessions. Another problem with introspective methods is that they are prone to distortions or blatant lies. Distortions may result from many causes and will probably be corrected when debugging the system. Outright lies are rare, thankfully, but signify a problem with the working relationship between the expert and knowledge engineer. A more serious criticism of the self-report is that mental phenomena are distorted by the very process of reporting. Loftus (1979) also casts doubt on the possibility of obtaining unbiased reports on internal events, since accurate reports of external events are problematic and tend to depend upon the observers' perspective. Alternatively, events which are reported may largely be illusory (Nisbet & Wilson 1977) owing to the lack of insight which the expert has on their method:

> People often cannot report accurately on the effects of particular stimuli on higher order, inference based responses. Indeed, sometimes they cannot report on the existence of critical stimuli, sometimes cannot report on the existence of their responses, and sometimes cannot even report that an inferential process of any kind has occurred (Nisbet & Wilson 1977, p. 233).

But the criticism was itself criticized (Smith & Miller 1978, Bainbridge 1979, Ericsson & Simon 1980), not only because many of the studies used by Nisbett & Wilson are not relevant to reasoning or problem solving but mostly because their review is highly selective and incomplete. They do not specify the circumstances when verbal report is accurate, and the qualifications of 'sometimes' and 'often' in their conclusion does not lead to any firm commitment.

Ericsson & Simon conclude that self-report need not interfere with the execution or performance of the task. Indeed, some evidence suggests that it may aid performance by making the reporter concentrate upon the reasoning. They also remark that self-report can be validated by other methods: the major and probably the only validation for knowledge engineers is the consistent performance of the expert system. The sources of invalidity or incompleteness in self-report are usually due to forgetting or the use of hypothetical rather than real situations. It is recognized that incompleteness is much more of a problem than invalidity, which is rarer (Breuker & Wielinga 1983). Incompleteness is likely when the knowledge underpinning the task performance is implicit and/or compiled. Invalidity often follows from incompleteness since omissions are replaced by post hoc justification or plausible explanations which lack the required attention to detail. Experts may have false theories as to how they actually perform the task and there will obviously be a conflict between the think-aloud data and the expert's incorrect model, with the experts strongly motivated to provide rationales to support their long-held belief of how they should solve a particular problem (Newell & Simon 1972). A complex task will also induce omissions owing to cognitive overload, which is solved by concentrating upon subtasks and allowing the expert to store partial results as notes.

Self-report is rarely a monologue. The knowledge engineer's presence will affect how the expert reports, and occasionally the expert will initiate a dialogue to explain a particular point or check that the process is being understood.

Nevertheless, think-aloud data has found a place in modern cognitive research and particularly in the domain of problem solving (Newell & Simon 1972). Of course there are differences between the requirements for building knowledge-based systems and psychological research. The psychologist is attempting to model cognitive processes, errors and problems included. The knowledge engineer uses think-aloud data as part of the task analysis and to achieve an understanding of the dynamic aspects of the domain. There is no constraint upon the knowledge engineer to improve upon the problem-solving techniques suggested by the think-aloud data. However, the approval of the expert should be sought before the knowledge engineer changes the method.

A psychological model to explain the process of self-report was set out by Elshout (1976). The central concept is 'working memory', which holds short-term task-related information, and although it has only a limited capacity it is not prone to interference. The important question is: How is working memory represented? If it is verbally coded then reporting will not interfere with the task. Otherwise, having to decode and translate the contents of working memory for verbalization will use up and possibly interfere with the working memory. Another issue is the relationship between working memory and long-term memory. The entire contents of working memory are accessible to self-report but there are limits to the amount of information obtainable from long-term memory, which is dependent upon cues and is prone to forgetfulness. Self-report is unlikely to reveal details of highly practised procedures which have become automated (Schneider & Shiffrin 1977). All that can be reported are the procedure calls. A refinement to the model is suggested by Breuker (1981) who makes the distinction between reasoning and inferencing, where reasoning consists of the successive application of operations on the content of working memory and inferencing consists of pattern-matching searches in long-term memory. The reasoning process is fed by and guides the inferential process. It is the reasoning processes that are reported in think-aloud protocols, but a full explanation is only achieved with an understanding of the inferential process.

Self-report is a very difficult technique despite all its beguiling simplicity. Experts find the comprehensive attention to detail aggravating. The knowledge engineers are unsure of how to deal with silences or when the expert provides an answer without an adequate explanation. Nevertheless, it still forms part of the knowledge engineer's toolkit and can provide information which no other technique could.

3.5 PERSONAL CONSTRUCTS AND KNOWLEDGE ENGINEERING

An example of technology transfer which will illustrate many of the effects of the interface between psychology and knowledge engineering is the repertory grid technique. The repertory grid technique was originally developed by Kelly (1955) as a method for unlocking an individually perceptual framework. Bainbridge (1979) has shown that there does not have to be a relationship between verbal reports and mental behaviour. The problem which faces the knowledge engineer — the problem which self-report attempts to address — is how to overcome cognitive defences that impede internal communication. Another solution is offered by personal construct psychology. Personal construct psychology provides a model of knowledge representation, acquisition and processing and may be used to develop the expert's vocabulary and encode the reasoning, encouraging the use of clear distinctions while applying the expertise, helping to structure the knowledge and identify and formulate the concepts.

In personal construct theory the primitive psychological unit is the construct or dichotomous distinction. The theory states that all human activity can be visualized as the anticipation of the future by construing the replication of events. Any inconsistencies between what the individual anticipated and the perceived reality cause changes to the individual's construct system.

Shaw & Gaines (1987) claim that personal construct theory provides cognitive foundations for knowledge elicitation and repertory grid techniques, including techniques for statistical analysis that provide a corresponding methodology. To provide an overall framework, Checkland's soft systems analysis is recommended (Checkland 1981). The systems analysis solves a major problem of the comparison between different construct systems. Similar construct systems may mean different things to their originators. Checkland's soft systems analysis begins with the proposition that very often there is no right answer and encourages the combination of contributions from a number of different persons. In personal construct terms this equates to the fuzzy combination of a number of different personal construct systems. Basden (1983) has investigated Checkland's soft systems analysis and reports favourably. In conclusion, Shaw & Gaines report that the methodology is easy to use, that the experts enjoy using the systems, but that the methodology is better suited for analysis rather than for synthesis, while causal and strategic knowledge is largely beyond the methodology. From a managerial point of view they suggest that the methodology can save at least two months' project calendar time. Without details of how such a finding was arrived at, it is difficult to comment, but this is the type of information which must be forthcoming before personal construct theory can be utilized as the basis for a practical methodology.

Personal construct theory was developed in the context of clinical psychology with the aim to bypass the subject's cognitive defences due to the therapist's probing. However, if the problem in knowledge engineering is intentional evasion rather than an unconscious cognitive defence mechanism then personal construct theory will be of little value since the expert will sabotage the knowledge elicitation process in other ways. If the problem is one of communication then personal construct theory may produce a result which is as unintelligible as any of the elicited explanations but without contextual information.

Personal construct theory has the most fervent supporters of any of the methods used by knowledge engineers — support that seems to have little relationship to its probable utility. It is difficult to reconcile Gammack's lukewarm review of the technique (above) with adherence to repertory grids to the almost total exclusion of any other elicitation techniques. Personal construct theory is also recommended as a basis for automatic elicitation (Shaw & Gaines 1986). Issues which are rarely considered are the effects of a repertory grid (or any other method) on the participants and the experts, including the experts' subjective opinions of the technique. Do they, for example, see the technique as alien and the result of the analysis contrary to their experience, and are the personal construct systems the results of post-rationalizations forced upon the expert? Hart (1986) is concerned about imposing alien tools and suggests that the experts should be encouraged to provide information in the most natural way for them. Any technique must also make explicit how it handles contextuality and implicit knowledge. The responsibility of proof rests upon the proponents of the repertory grid techniques. My largely unfounded opinion is that repertory grids have a place in knowledge engineering when the need arises in domains in which the conceptual structure is complex, limited in scope and without a clear nomenclature. This may be doing the technique an injustice. It is likely that experience shall be the judge, not experimentation.

3.6 INTERVIEWS

Many of the techniques which have been assessed are derived from psychological research. One technique which is common to many social sciences and everyday life is the interview. Knowledge elicitation, discounting automatic techniques or qualitative or structure-based methods (e.g. cardsort), consists very largely of interviewing. Knowledge engineering must use a far wider range of techniques than just interviewing. Nevertheless, interviewing is so central to knowledge elicitation either independently or in conjunction with another method of data collection that it is difficult to evaluate its true worth.

The psychologist uses interviews to collect accounts, while knowledge engineers are interested in explanations and, to a lesser extent, facts. Explanations include justifications, theories and anecdotal examples. However, there is a rough equivalence between the explanations from knowledge elicitation and the accounts or narratives collected by psychologists. Many knowledge engineers have been mystified by the amount of anecdotal material which their experts use to explain a point. Cohler (1982) considers narratives the most internally consistent of presently understood past, experienced present and anticipated future methods of communication. The narrative is a natural way to communicate information, and the more complex the information the more likely it is that narratives will be used. The interview which is oriented towards collecting the narrative is an important part of knowledge engineering. The narrative has therefore an important part to play in knowledge engineering (Kornell 1988). Kornell makes an important distinction between two different types of thought. The first is what he describes as 'formal' or 'logical' thought such as that found in science and mathematics. The second type of thought is 'narrative' thought. This is most typically the sort of thought which knowledge engineers encounter in the form of metaphors and analogies. An expert system which operates at the level of narrative thought must model the patterns of reasoning used by the expert as well as facts and heuristics. The current generation of knowledge acquisition tools fails to identify or represent the patterns of expert reasoning which Kornell believes are so important.

The psychology of the interview is mostly concerned with two issues. The first is an analysis of verbal reports: we must include here the analysis of think-aloud protocols. The work of Ericsson & Simon (1984) is authoritative here, although only a small proportion of their work is directly relevant to knowledge elicitation. The second issue is the dynamics of the interview itself and the analysis of qualitative data in the form of explanations and justifications of domain knowledge rather than attempts to describe problem-solving behaviour.

An interview is a joint production of what the interviewer and respondents talk about and how they talk about it (Mishler 1986). To be more specific, interviews are speech events comprising discourse, constructed jointly by the participants, the analysis and interpretation of which is based on a theory of discourse and meaning. The theory of discourse is culturally specific while the meaning of questions and answers is contextually grounded and, in knowledge-engineering terms, very largely domain-specific. This qualitative interview eliminates any analysis based on some form of coding and statistics which is favoured in much of psychological research. However, alternative analyses are generally perceived as unscientific by many psychologists. The assumption is, of course, that knowledge acquisition/engineering is also unscientific.

Maccoby & Maccoby (1954) describe an interview as the face-to-face verbal interchange in which one person (the interviewer) attempts to elicit information or expressions of opinion or belief from one or more persons. Interviewing is a special form of human interaction with a specific purpose and context area which attempts to eliminate any extraneous information. The interview is a pattern of interaction in which the roles of the interviewer and respondent are highly specialized and specific.

Kahn & Cannell (1957) suggest that the important factors which influence the outcome of an interview include the emphasis of a question, whether it is positive, negative, neutral, directive or non-directive; the order of questions; and specific social attributes such as the sex, expectations and attitudes of the participants.

Even in a tightly controlled psychology experiment the relationship between the question to be asked and what actually is asked is not straightforward. Bremner (1982) reported that interviewers altered one-third of the questions during the interview, this claim being supported by other researchers (Bradburn & Sudman 1979, Cannell *et al.* 1975). This and the finding by Molenaar (1982) that wording variations in the questions and the order in which the questions are asked have significant effects throw doubt on the validation of serial interviews as a complementary methodology in psychology. Of course knowledge engineering is very different — even in multiple-expert situations the experts are not surveyed but their respective contributions are combined supplementally. However, knowledge engineers cannot be complacent. These studies show that interviews are prone to many forces and the planned question may not resemble the question which was actually asked. Hence the need for audio recordings at least. The techniques and style of the interviewer are meant to bridge the gap between asking and answering. The consequences of the gap are virtually unpredictable but represent a real possibility of bias and lack of accuracy in the knowledge analysis. The process of audio tape transcription is another area where research findings have discovered errors and inaccuracies. Isaacs (1986) observed after re-listening to the original audio recordings that the typists filtered out items of special significance. Isaacs wanted to understand her respondents' personal lives rather than know how they operated in their professional lives, but the problem of poor or selective transcription will almost certainly have an affect in knowledge engineering.

Within the interview there are a number of psychological effects. The lack of motivation is one particular problem in knowledge elicitation. Relatively informal studies of the interviews have suggested the following tell-tale signs of poor motivation on behalf of the expert. The signs of low motivation can be very subtle since the overriding consideration is for the rules of conversational cooperation (Grice 1975). Poor motivation may well be expressed as a form of cooperation but a form which is less than required to complete the particular phase of the project, an example being underreporting — giving short simple replies when deeper explanations were required. It is not easy to know if the expert is telling less than he knows, but unexplained silences, vague and general statements and monosyllabic answers are strong symptoms of underreporting (Breuker & Wielinga 1983b). The expert may take initiatives which are more properly the domain of the knowledge engineer, or concentrate on personal or alternative work needs. Finally, a lack of motivation may be manifested by a propensity to be distracted.

Motivational factors can be either intrinsically or extrinsically motivated (Kahn & Cannell 1957). Intrinsic factors are contained within the interview or project while extraneous factors are outside the scope of the project. Expert motivation is enhanced when a large number of motivational factors are present and factors which cause lack of motivation are decreased. The knowledge engineer has most control over intrinsic factors such as complying with the usual conventions of communication, providing an ethos of critical but non-judgemental understanding, and recognizing the expert's valuable contribution and role. Extrinsic factors which effect the expert's motivational states are the rewards which follow from participation and a successful project, and the enthusiasm from sharing the common goals with the knowledge engineer and others.

As with any social situation the personalities of the participants are a determinant of the outcome, but to what extent is questionable. The effect of personalities on the project is very likely to be swamped by other factors (e.g. social pressure for meaningful communication). However, personality clashes can be detrimental to the project, thus distorting the paths of communication between the knowledge engineer and the expert. Symptoms of this distortion range from the wilful and belligerent breakdown of communication to the less than adequate degree of specificity required by the knowledge engineer. Belligerence, thankfully, is rare in knowledge-engineering projects.

The knowledge engineer has a choice of structured or unstructured interviews (for a detailed description of structured interviews see Breuker & Wielinga 1984). Lofland (1971) believes that the structured interview is most suitable when the interviewer knows 'what the important questions are and more importantly what the main kind of answers can be' (p. 75), whereas the unstructured interview is suitable when the interviewer wishes to be flexible with the specific subject matter. It is more a technique to discover information by guiding the respondent to give rich and detailed information which must be analysed qualitatively. In knowledge-engineering terms that means developing an understanding.

Kuipers & Kassirer (1987) perform a case study to examine the analysis techniques of verbal protocols using a physician as the expert. This is an attempt to place the interview within a knowledge-engineering context using specific analytical techniques. They desire 'a methodology of discovery to determine the constraints from human behaviour that help us develop adequate hypotheses about the structure of knowledge representations' (p. 47). As opposed to psychological enquiry based upon a specific population, the methodology of discovery provides the richness of data needed to investigate the complexity of human knowledge.

Their research consists of an expert/subject talking-through problem-solving activity (medical diagnosis) based on a detailed printed description of a patient. There are two goals to the analysis — firstly, identifying objects and relations, and secondly, identifying the causal relations. The types of analyses investigated include referring phrase analysis in which conceptual objects are identified; assertional analysis follows up the details of those objects which are identified in referring phrase analysis, and script analysis identifies the overall structure of the reasoning process. Representing the problem-solving activity follows from the refinements of the analyses. A knowledge representation is developed to represent the qualitative structure of the problem-solving mechanism. Any knowledge representation must be judged by ascertaining what states of knowledge can be represented and what inferences can take place. Kuipers & Kassirer appear to be advocating the handcrafting of expert systems through detailed analysis of expert behaviour. The software follows directly from the knowledge analysis: the interviews are tailored to elicit the data required by the analysis techniques.

Belkin *et al.* (1988) perform a similar research project, concentrating upon analysis of interview data rather than the interview itself. They study discourse analysis coupled with observation in what they term an informational provision environment. The interviews were audio-recorded and the tapes transcribed and analysed in great detail, utterance by utterance. The analysis techniques include assigning utterances to prespecified functional categories, identifying the purposes of each utterance, ascertaining what knowledge would be required to make the utterance and, finally, categorizing the utterances. This initial research is meant to lead towards an intelligent document retrieval system. Their research led to the minimum number of functions required for the document retrieval system although this can only be substantiated by a working system.

3.7 METHODOLOGICAL CHOICE

The major problem in knowledge engineering is not only a question of which techniques are better than others but of which methodology or conceptual framework is better and for what domains.

Breuker & Wielinga's Knowledge Acquisition and Documentation Structuring (KADS) is a methodology and a tool which supports the methodology. Breuker & Wielinga (1987) take a simple and direct approach to the problem of efficient knowledge acquisition and knowledge analysis by beginning with an analysis of problem-solving behaviour itself. This is a logical starting point. After all, the object of study is the understanding of domain-specific problem solving, and the implication is that the reasoning underpinning successful problem solving is related to the reasoning underpinning successful knowledge acquisition and implementation. Furthermore, this reasoning can be formalized into a methodology.

The first major principle of problem solving is that it is far easier to solve complex problems if they are partitioned into a number of less complex problems. Further partition, if needed, and the solution of relatively simple subproblems is a structured approach. Problem solving and knowledge engineering should specify how to decompose major problems into manageable subproblems. A second principle of efficient problem solving suggests that a problem should be analysed as fully as possible before possible solutions are tested or applied. It is wise to know exactly what the problem is if it is to be solved and also to have as much relevant data as possible. Therefore the methodology of building expert systems must emphasize a full analysis before any coding takes place. The techniques of knowledge analysis are performed in a semiparallel fashion, slowly building up the overall picture of the nature of the expertise.

The crucial stage in the knowledge analysis is the intermediate step between problem identification and the selection of solutions. This stage involves the interpretation of the knowledge analysis with reference to a coherent framework or model.

Breuker & Wielinga distinguish two major functions of knowledge acquisition. The first is the elicitation of data pertaining to domain knowledge. The components of domain knowledge include the domain vocabulary, an outline of the relevant problems and typical tasks which the expert solves, and examples of the solutions which would result from the investigation. The second major function of knowledge acquisition is the analysis of verbal data or, more accurately, the transformation of verbal data into an interpretative framework.

Expert systems are built in three stages. The first is the orientation stage, the acquisition of domain vocabulary being the most important function of this stage. The second stage, problem identification, includes the analysis of domain concepts, a functional analysis of the proposed system, the ultimate solution to the current knowledge-engineering problem and a task analysis of the expertise. The third and most complex stage is the problem analysis, including an analysis of the user and the operational environment and, most importantly, a detailed analysis of the dynamic expertise.

Central to Breuker & Wielinga's methodology is the concept of the interpretation model. An interpretation model is required in order to make sense of the mountain of data which the knowledge engineer collects during interviews with the expert. Those aspects of the domain analysis that are stable and sufficiently specific are used to build the interpretation model. The psychological analysis of problem solving reveals a core of domain-independent systematic problem-solving techniques that underpin the domain-specific knowledge. Consequently, they suggest that the task structure is a good point of departure for designing interpretation models.

Interpretation models have a number of functions. They can be 'used to assist communication between the knowledge engineer and the expert, for checking the completeness of data or, most importantly, to facilitate the mapping of the information (which is encapsulated in the model) to the formalism used for the knowledge representation'. In other words, an interpretation model may be used as an efficient and comprehensive intermediate representation.

Breuker & Wielinga identify five different levels of interpretation. The first level is knowledge identification, which is mostly an analysis of domain terms. The second level is knowledge conceptualization in which the individual domain concepts are integrated according to a number of abstract or conceptual primitives, such as is-a and part-of, which relate objects. The third and most important level is the epistemological analysis. This uncovers the structural properties of the expertise — more of this below. The fourth level is the logical analysis in which structures are mapped onto formalisms for expressing the knowledge and inferencing. This is part of the design stage. The final level is the implementation analysis, the stage at which the knowledge is represented in programmatic terms in accordance with the specific knowledge representation language.

The epistemological level is important for two reasons. Firstly, the jump from linguistic data to the implementational level is too great to be completed in one step. Secondly, avoiding the epistemological level may result in an unstructured and opaque system with the strong possibility that information will be lost. The epistemological level is the level at which interpretation models are constructed from the five primitive types: objects, knowledge sources — a set of knowledge that infers new objects from given objects —

models such as causal models or processes, structures such as hierarchies, and finally, strategies, which are high-level plans for invoking the problem-solving knowledge sources. An interpretation model is a generic model of the problem-solving processes for a particular class of tasks.

The KADS methodology has been tested in a number of domains, but few, if any, working commercial systems have been constructed using the methodology. However, it represents the most detailed attempt to construct a methodology for building expert systems from a psychological perspective. Unfortunately, it is complex, and perhaps unwieldy, because it aims to be comprehensive and functional. The methodology needs a number of commercial applications to tighten up the practical side.

Compare KADS, based on problem-solving theory and principles, with cognitive emulation based on the hypothesized workings on the mind. Slatter (1987) couples a cognitive perspective with a pragmatic orientation to formulate a practical methodology for building expert systems. Cognitive emulation refers to a style of expert system which emulates human thinking. The guiding principle is to model the way the expert actually represents the knowledge as well as the expert's and users' cognitive processes. It is not assumed that cognitive emulation is applicable to all domains, so Slatter recommends a feasibility study to investigate the viability of the strategy. Few other authors mention the role of the feasibility study in their writings, although the orientation stage in KADS is largely concerned with a feasibility study. Practical experience (Greenwell 1988) suggests that the feasibility study is one of the most important functions in an expert system project.

Evidence from psychological studies of cognitive processes and expertise point to the domain specificity of cognitive procedures. This finding is largely derived from the numerous studies of expert/novice comparisons. A second finding is the development of pattern matching and memory skills in the expert's cognitive procedures. Two levels of explanation seem to prevail. Firstly, expertise is the result of the development of the brain's natural functionality — more specifically, highly parallel and pattern-oriented processing. Secondly, at a higher level there seems to be the strategic ability to reflect upon and adapt problem-solving strategies. Slatter concludes that too little is known of how largely automated cognitive skills and strategic thinking, which consciously controls the cognitive level, are combined. This is the priority for research, and not comparisons between groups such as experts and novices.

There are a number of problems with cognitive emulation. The most important is that it would directly model the bad points of human cognition — the ability to make simple and silly errors or forget vital information, as well as whatever it is that makes people innovative problem solvers. A true representation of human problem solving from a cognitive perspective may be inefficient or inapplicable. A further problem is reconciling the cognitive processes of a number of experts when more than one expert is required to complete the project.

On the positive side cognitive emulation and knowledge engineering seem inseparable, and as Slatter emphasizes, cognitive emulation provides a principled approach to expert system design. However, effective knowledge elicitation which utilizes psychologically oriented techniques does not support cognitive emulation as Slatter suggests. Neither can the case be made that cognitive emulation promotes user acceptance. True, user acceptance is very much a psychological issue, but for commercial reasons it is more probably a question of ergonomics and effective training and communication. The applicability of cognitive emulation is constrained by cognitive processes which are not amenable to emulation or fall outside known psychological understanding.

Therefore cognitive emulation is perhaps one consideration, but somehow it can never get very far because it directs the knowledge engineer away from the domain and towards the functioning of the mind. Expert systems are representations of domain knowledge first and foremost, whether or not this is erroneous, and representations of mental functions secondly if at all. The work described by Les Johnson and colleagues is another attempt to move the analysis away from the domain and towards what makes an expert an expert.

The knowledge acquisition methodology suggested by Johnson & Johnson (1987) has three major characteristics. Firstly, Pask's conversation theory (Pask 1974) is the theoretical basis of the knowledge elicitation technique known as teachback. Secondly, the methodological keynote is building expert systems which demonstrate competence rather than behavioural correctness. Finally, the knowledge acquisition procedure is strongly oriented towards semistructured interviews with a detailed analysis of the transcripts.

The starting point for an analysis of the Johnsons' contribution to expert system technology is undoubtedly the notion of competence, which appears to be present only in the work of Les Johnson either singly or in collaboration with others (Keravnou & Johnson 1986, Johnson & Johnson 1987). Competence is contrasted against a more traditional view of 'as good as expert performance', where this refers to a more procedural system. A competence-based system is more conceptually based. A competent problem solver structures factual knowledge in the most effective and efficient way to apply problem-solving heuristics. The closer a system models competence the greater is its acceptance in the work place environment. Competence has three components: strategies, structures and dialogue.

Pask's conversation theory is concerned with the understanding between two people of the process by which entities are made objective and mutually understood. Consequently, the detailed analysis of the interview between the knowledge engineer and the expert is central to the knowledge analysis. The analysis of verbal interaction is at two levels. Level 0 consists of the procedures and algorithms which create relations, and level 1 consists of the methods by which the level 0 procedures are constructed.

The meta-level (level 1) relates to how specific procedures are stored in memory and recalled when needed. The teachback-interviewing technique is quite simply the expert explaining a procedure to the knowledge engineer and the knowledge engineer communicating back an understanding of it to the expert. When the expert is satisfied they move on to another topic. The explanation given by the expert is at level 0 and through teachback this is converted into level 1 knowledge.

The teachback method is designed to elicit both global and specific structures and to reduce the amount of bias arising from the interviewer's preconceptions about the domain. The knowledge engineer's understanding is immediately verified by the expert. Johnson & Johnson also claim that their method is a non-psychological and non-judgemental technique which encourages good interview practice, making efficient use of the expert's time. However, teachback is not a strongly structured technique so it requires much general interview training and presumably some practice. There is a high cognitive load on the knowledge engineer during the interviews and much time is taken up with transcription.

3.8 INDUCTION

KADS, cognitive emulation and competence represent just a selection of the possible ways to approach an expert systems project. They have been included largely because of the psychological basis of the methodologies. With these and other competing methodologies and techniques the reader may wish for an alternative, hopefully automatic, method of acquiring and representing knowledge. One candidate for the automation of the processes is induction. One possible solution is to model or simulate the process of induction. As with the personal construct theory the motivation for using induction is the difficulty of eliciting private knowledge. This may be because the expert has never been asked to formulate his decision-making and problem-solving processes. An objective method — which induction must be if it is truly induction — would avoid distortion due to human intervention and the particular technique used.

Induction means an induction algorithm. The ID3 algorithm (Quinlan 1979) creates a decision tree of rules from a training set of examples. Abstracted from the training set are a number of attributes whose values are thought to have significant effects on decision making and final outcomes. The decision tree represents an explanation of any underlying pattern and is used to predict the results of examples not in the training set. The algorithm will fail if there are contradictions or errors in the training set. In evaluating ID3, Hart (1987) used the past decisions of a college admissions tutor as the basis for a training set — a domain which she recognizes is probably too simple to really test ID3.

The creation of the training set is not a trivial exercise; this can be a disadvantage to the method. Examples must be carefully selected so that rare outcomes are included and superfluous or contradictory examples omitted. A certain degree of domain knowledge will be required to select the attributes. The results of the algorithm are usually checked, so some recognition is made between the output and what the expert actually does.

The knowledge engineer must be careful not to impose a solution on the program by artificially manipulating and massaging the data as well as interpreting the output. It is obvious that induction must be tested on some realistic problems. Also, there is no guarantee that the output is applicable to cases other than those which were included in the training set.

Perhaps one of Hart's (1987) most telling comments is that 'Induction is unlikely to answer all questions, but it may highlight interesting or difficult cases' (p. 178). It will be some time before we can have estimates of how many questions induction will answer. If it is the case that the power of inductive algorithms is limited, why should we go through the convoluted process at all? If a knowledge engineer is trained to work with psychological phenomena, surely the recognition of interesting or difficult cases would be a part of their everyday analysis.

The expert does not have a lot of confidence in induced rules, regarding them as in some way foreign. As Wellbank (1983) has said, 'As long as machine induction produces rules which split the domain up in different ways from those the expert uses it has serious limitations as a knowledge elicitation method' (p. 48). Induced rules can be easy to understand and unnatural at the same time and since they come without explanation have to be taken on faith. Those domains which are suitable for induction include pattern recognition and fault diagnosis, while real time problems are less suitable. The main advantage induction has over other methods of knowledge acquisition is the possible discovery of rules that the expert was unaware of. A commercial advantage is that the software is designed to be used by the expert alone. The major use for induction, currently, is as the basis for consultation with the expert. Without any detailed study of the time it takes to complete the interaction with inductive software compared to other methods, it is difficult to really evaluate the current role of induction in knowledge engineering. On the cautious side it appears that the best use of inductive software is as an adjunct to other methods of knowledge engineering. More optimistically, the improvements in the software and a development of a methodology which includes induction as a major technique could be available in the not too distant future.

Knowledge engineering is the result of psychological research and has been advanced largely by psychologists. However, psychological research and commercial considerations are at best uneasy bedfellows and at worst totally incompatible. Sometimes it appears the researcher is not looking for a solution to a problem or a better way of doing things but is constantly plugging a pet idea or theory in the most blinkered fashion. At other times methodological complexities and philosophies are created which appear to be more difficult to understand than any domain of expertise which the knowledge engineer will ever work upon.

To end on a positive note, it is nevertheless comforting to know that research is undertaken no matter how abstract, abstruse or tangential it is to immediate practical concerns, and that eventually there will be an integration between formal research findings and practical experience.

REFERENCES

Bainbridge, L. (1979) Verbal reports as evidence of the process operator's knowledge. *International Journal of Man–Machine Studies* **11** (4) 411–436

Basden, A. (1983) On the application of expert systems. *International Journal of Man–Machine Studies* **19** (5) 461–477

Belkin, N. J., Brooks, H. M., & Daniels, P. J. (1988) Knowledge elicitation using discourse analysis. In: Gaines, B., & Boose, J. (eds) *Knowledge acquisition for knowledge-based systems*. Academic Press, London

Boden, M. A. (1988) *Computer models of mind*. Cambridge University Press, Cambridge

Bradburn, M. M., & Sudman, S. (1979) *Improving interview method and questionnaire design*. Jossey-Bass, San Francisco, CA

Bremner, M. (1982) Response effects of 'role-restricted' characteristics of the interviewer. In: Dijkstra, W., & van der Zouwen, J. (eds) *Response behaviour in the survey interview*. Academic Press, New York

Breuker, J. A. (1981) Availability of knowledge. COWO, University of Amsterdam

Breuker, J. A., & Wielinga, B. J. (1983a) Analysis techniques for knowledge based systems, Part 1, Report 1.1, Esprit Project 12. Memorandum 28 of the research project 'The acquisition of expertise', University of Amsterdam

Breuker, J. A., & Wielinga, B. J. (1983b) Analysis techniques for knowledge based systems, Report 1.2, Esprit Project 12. Memorandum 28 of the research Project 'The acquisition of expertise', University of Amsterdam

Breuker, J. A., & Wielinga, B. J. (1984) Techniques for knowledge elicitation and analysis, Report 1.5, Esprit Project 12. Memorandum 28 of the research project 'The Acquisition of expertise', University of Amsterdam

Breuker, J. A., & Wielinga, B. J. (1987) Use of models in the interpretation of verbal data. In: Kidd, A. L. (ed.) *Knowledge acquisition for expert systems: a practical handbook*. Plenum Press, New York

Bruner, J. S., Goodnow, J., & Austin, G. (1956) *A study of thinking*. Wiley, New York

Buhler, K. (1908) Tatsache und Probleme zu einer Psychologie der Denkvorgaenge: II. Ueber Gedankenzusammenhaenge; III. Ueber Gedankenerrinnerungen. *Archiv fuer die Gesamte Psychologie* **12** 1–92

Cannell, C. F., Lawson, S. A., & Hausser, D. L. (1975) *A technique for evaluating interview performance*. Survey Research Centre of the Institute of Social Research, University of Michigan Ann Arbor, MI

Card, S. K., Moran, T. P., & Newell, A. (1983) *The psychology of human–computer interaction*. Erlbaum, Hilldale, NJ.

Checkland, P. (1981) *Systems thinking, systems practice*. Wiley, Chichester

Cleaves, D. A. (1988) Cognitive biases and corrective techniques; proposals for improving elicitation procedures for knowledge-based systems. In: Gaines, B., & Boose, J. (eds) *Knowledge acquisition for knowledge-based systems*. Academic Press, London

Cohler, J. B. (1982) Personal narrative and life course. In: Baltes, P. B., &

Brim, O. J. Jr (eds) *Life-span development and behaviour* vol. 4. Academic Press, New York

Cragan, J., & Wright, D. (1980) *Communication in small group discussions: a case study approach*. West Publishing Company, New York

Doyle, J. (1983) Methodological simplicity in expert systems construction: the case of judgements and reasoned assumptions. *AI Magazine* **4** (2) 39–43

Eisenson, J., Auer, J., & Irwin, J. (1963) *The psychology of communication*. Appleton-Century-Crofts, New York

Elshout, J. J. (1976) *Karakteristieke moeilijkheden bij het denken*. University of Amsterdam

Ericsson, K. A., & Simon, H. A. (1980) Verbal reports as data. *Psychological Review* **87** (3) 215–251

Ericsson, K. A., & Simon, H. A. (1984) *Protocol analysis: verbal report as data*. MIT Press, Cambridge MA

Flanagan, J. C. (1954) The critical incident technique. *Psychological Bulletin* **51** 327–358

Fox, J., Myers, C. D., Greaves, M. F., & Pegram, S. (1987) A systematic study of knowledge base refinement in the diagnosis of leukemia. In: Kidd, A. L. (ed.), *Knowledge acquisition for expert systems: a practical handbook*. Plenum Press New York

Gaines, B. R. (1988) An overview of knowledge-acquisition and transfer. In: Gaines, B. R., & Boose, J. (eds) *Knowledge acquisition for knowledge-based systems*. Academic Press, London

Gammack, J. G. (1987) Different techniques and different aspects on declarative knowledge. In: Kidd, A. L. (ed.), *Knowledge acquisition for expert systems: a practical handbook*. Plenum Press, New York

Greenwell, M. R. (1988) *Knowledge engineering for expert systems*. Ellis Horwood, Chichester

Grice, H. P. (1975) Logic and conversation. In: Cole, P., & Morgan, J. L. (eds) *Syntax and semantics, volume III, speech acts*. Academic Press, New York

Hart, A. (1986) *Knowledge acquisition for expert systems*. Kogan Page, London

Hart, A. (1987) Role of induction in knowledge elicitation. In: Kidd, A. L. (ed.) *Knowledge acquisition for export systems: a practical handbook*. Plenum Press, New York

Huseman, R. (1973) The role of the nominal group in small group communication. In: Huseman, R., Logue, D. M., & Freshley, D. L. (eds), *Readings in interpersonal and organisational communication*. 2nd ed. Hollbrook, Boston, MA

Isaacs, L. (1986) Personal communication reported in: Mishler, E. G. *Research interviewing: context and narrative*. Harvard University Press, Cambridge, MA

Johnson, L., & Johnson, N. E. (1987) Knowledge elicitation involving teachback interviewing. In: Kidd, A. L. (ed.) *Knowledge acquisition for export systems: a practical handbook*. Plenum Press, New York

Johnson-Laird, P. N. (1983) *Mental models: towards a cognitive science of language, inference and consciousness.* Cambridge University Press, Cambridge

Kahn, R. L., & Cannell, C. F. (1957) *The dynamics of interviewing: theory techniques and cases.* Wiley, New York

Kassirer, J. P., & Gorry, G. A. (1978) Clinical problem solving: a behavioural analysis. *Annals of Internal Medicine* **89** (2) 245–255

Kelly, G. A. (1955) *The psychology of personal constructs.* Norton, New York

Keravnou, E. T., & Johnson, L. (1986) *Competent expert systems: a case study in fault diagnosis.* Kogan Page, London

Kidd, A. L. (1987) Knowledge acquisition — an introductory framework. In: Kidd, A. L. (ed.), *Knowledge acquisition for expert systems: a practical handbook.* Plenum Press New York

Kidd, A. L., & Cooper, M. B. (1983) Man-machine interface for an expert system. Presented at 3rd British Computer Society Conference on Expert Systems, Cambridge University.

Kleinmuntz, B. (1968) The processing of clinical information by man and machine. In: Kleinmuntz, B. (ed.) *Formal representation of human judgement.* Wiley, New York

Kornell, J. (1988) Formal thought and narrative thought in knowledge acquisition. In: Gaines, B. R., & Boose, J. (eds) *Knowledge acquisition for knowledge-based systems* Academic Press, London

Kuipers, B., & Kassirer, J. P. (1987) Knowledge acquisition by analysis of verbatim protocols. In: Kidd, A. L. (ed.) *Knowledge acquisition for expert systems: a practical handbook.* Plenum Press, New York

Lofland, J. (1971) *Analysing social settings.* Wadsworth, Belmont, CA

Loftus, E. (1979) *Eyewitness testimony.* Harvard University Press, Cambridge, MA

Maccoby, E. E., & Maccoby, N. (1954) The interview: a tool of social science. In: Lindzey, G. (ed.), *Handbook of social psychology.* vol. 1. Addison-Wesley, Cambridge, MA

McGraw, K. L., & Seale, M. R. (1988) Knowledge elicitation with multiple experts: considerations and techniques. *AI Review* **2** (1)

Miller, G. A., Galanter, E., & Pribram, K. H. (1960) *Plans and the structure of behaviour.* Holt, Rinehart & Wilson, New York

Mishler, E. G. (1986) *Research interviewing: context and narrative.* Harvard University Press, Cambridge MA

Molenaar, N. J. (1982) Response effects of 'formal' characteristics of questions. In: Dijkstra, W., & van der Zouwen, J. (eds) *Response behaviour in the survey interview.* Academic Press, New York

Newell, A., Shaw, J. C., & Simon, H. A. (1957) Empirical explorations with the logic theory machine. *Proceedings of the Western Joint Computer Conference* vol. 15, pp. 218–39. Reprinted in: Feigenbaum, E. A., & Feldman, J. (eds) (1963) *Computers and thought.* McGraw-Hill, New York

Newell, A., & Simon, H. A. (1961) GPS — a program that simulates human thought. In: Biling, H. (ed.), *Lernende Automaten.* Oldenbourg, Munich.

Reprinted in; Feigenbaum, E. A., & Feldman, J. (eds) (1963) *Computers and thought*. McGraw-Hill, New York

Newell, A., & Simon, H. A. (1972) *Human problem solving*. Prentice-Hall, Englewood Cliffs, NJ

Nisbet, R. E., & Wilson, T. D. (1977) Telling more than we know: verbal reports on mental processes. *Psychological Review* **84** 231–59

Osborn, A. (1953) *Applied imagination: principles and procedures of creative thinking*. Scribner, New York

Pask, G. (1974) *Conversation, cognition and learning: a cybernetic theory and methodology*. Elsevier, London

Quinlan, R. (1979) Discovering rules from large collections of examples: a case study. In: Michie, D. (ed.) *Expert systems in the microelectronic age*. Edinburgh University Press, Edinburgh

Schneider, W., & Shiffrin, R. M. (1977) Automatic and controlled information processing in vision. In: Laberge, D., & Samuels, S. J. (eds) *Basic processes in reading*. Lawrence Erlbaum, Hillsdale, NJ

Schweickert, R., Burton, A. M., Taylor, N. K., Corlett, E. N., Shadbolt, N. R., & Hedgecock, A. P. (1987) Comparing knowledge elicitation techniques: a case study. *AI Review* **1** 245–253

Shaw, M. E. (1932) A comparison of individuals and small groups in the rational solution of complex problems. *American Journal of Psychology* **44** 491–504

Shaw, M. L. G., & Gaines, B. R. (1986) Interactive elicitation of knowledge from experts. *Future Computing Systems* **1** (2) 151–90

Shaw, M. L. G., & Gaines, B. R. (1987) An interactive knowledge elicitation technique using personal construct technology. In: Kidd, A. L. (ed.), *Knowledge acquisition for expert systems: a practical handbook*. Plenum Press, New York

Shweder, R. A. (1977) Likeness and likelihood in everyday thought: magical thinking and everyday judgements about personality. In: Johnson-Laird, P. N., & Wason, P. C. (eds) *Thinking: readings in cognitive science*. Cambridge University Press, Cambridge

Slater, P. (1958) Contrasting correlates of group size. *Sociometry* **25** 129–39

Slatter, P. E. (1987) *Building expert systems: cognitive emulation*. Ellis Horwood, Chichester

Smith, E. R., & Miller, F. D. (1978) Limits on perception of cognitive processes: a reply to Nisbett and Wilson. *Psychological Review* **85** 355–62

Spetzler, G. S., & Stael Von Holstein, C. S. (1975) Probability encoding in decision analysis. *Management Science* **22** (3) 340–58

Steiner, I. (1972) *Group process and productivity*. Academic Press, New York

Tversky, A., & Kahnemann, D. (1974) Judgement under uncertainty: heuristics and biases. *Science* **125** 1124–31

Wason, P. C., & Johnson-Laird, P. N. (1972) *Psychology of reasoning: structure and content*. B. T. Batsford, London

Wellbank, M. (1983) A review of knowledge acquisition techniques for expert systems. Memorandum No. R19/022/83, British Telecom Research Laboratories, Martlesham Heath, Ipswich

4

The representation and use of knowledge

Brendan McGee

4.1 INTRODUCTION

Since the development of electronic computers in the 1950s, computers have generally been used to automate a range of tasks which, although often complex and time-consuming, are characterized by their routine and repetitive nature. These tasks are well-suited to solutions based on algorithmic methods. The key to the efficient implementation of algorithmic computer systems is based on *data*-structuring techniques, i.e. defining data structures which facilitates the processing which is to be carried out on the data.

The trend in recent years of using computers to solve problems which, in contrast, are knowledge-intensive and non-algorithmic in nature has prompted the development of alternative computer systems — expert or knowledge-based systems. Unlike conventional systems, the key to the efficient implementation of knowledge-based systems is *knowledge* structuring, i.e. defining a suitable representation for the problem-solving knowledge incorporated in the system.

The theme of this chapter is knowledge representation. Whereas conventional data structuring concentrates on efficient techniques for representing numerical data and file records, knowledge representation is concerned with the efficient representation of everyday concepts, situations and common-sense knowledge found within the application domain of the knowledge-based system. The unique demands of the knowledge representation problem have prompted the development of a number of different representation paradigms, each of which addresses the representation of everyday concepts and commonsense knowledge in a particular way.

In this chapter we first discuss the two types of knowledge which are typically employed by an expert during the problem-solving process. We then present some common representations for these types of knowledge typically found in commercial expert system development tools. We show how these paradigms are used to represent expert knowledge in practical situations through the use of simple examples.

4.2 HEURISTIC AND DESCRIPTIVE KNOWLEDGE

Problems which are tackled by experts are typically difficult and poorly understood. Usually it is not possible to solve them by following a methodical or well-formulated procedure. One of the things which differentiates an expert from others in his field is his ability, when faced with a specific problem, to apply a problem-solving strategy which leads him quickly to an acceptable solution for the problem.

The knowledge which allows experts to deliver performance at consistently high levels takes many forms. One identifiable part of their knowledge is the background knowledge for their particular domains of expertise. Background knowledge in a particular field can be gained through formal study of textbooks or by attending lectures. Typically this is how students begin to acquire knowledge when they decide to learn a particular discipline. Having successfully completed a course of study, the student emerges with a new vocabulary consisting of specific terms relevant to the discipline and a formal theory for the field represented by definitions, axioms or mathematical laws and equations. However, graduating students are not normally considered to be experts. Typically, they are able to describe the knowledge they have acquired but encounter difficulties in applying the knowledge to solve practical problems.

This indicates that there is another dimension to expertise, one which cannot be fulfilled through formal study. Formal theories can provide explanations for phenomena which occur in a domain but provide little guidance in applying this knowledge to solve a given problem. Problem-solving knowledge is normally acquired through experience and represents an important part of the expert's ability. The form of this knowledge is quite different to formal background knowledge.

Problem-solving techniques applied by the expert often have no formal basis but are based on observations and empirical associations gathered by the expert over time. On the basis of his experience, the expert develops rules of thumb which allow him to focus his attention on the key aspects of a problem which will lead him quickly to a solution. These rules of thumb are often called *heuristics* and this type of knowledge is often called *heuristic* knowledge.

4.2.1 Heuristic knowledge

Heuristic knowledge is generally considered to be 'shallow', i.e. heuristics ignore the formally expressed laws and relationships which make up the theory of a problem domain. They simply express surface relationships which an expert has observed to be of use when tackling problems in the domain. They can often be stated in the form of rules. For example, an expert car mechanic may use the following heuristic when diagnosing starting problems with a car:

> If the engine doesn't start and the starter turns the engine normally, and there is no spark at the spark plugs, then the problem is probably in the ignition circuit.

This motor diagnosis heuristic states a relationship between an engine, a starter and an ignition circuit. However, it does not refer to the functionality of these components (which could be expressed in quite agonizing detail in terms of mathematical models for example). Through experience, the mechanic will have noted the surface relationship between these components and will quite happily forget, for the present at least, the detailed knowledge that he has about the underlying functionality of the components. The surface relationship provides him with sufficient information to carry out the diagnosis task efficiently while ignoring the wealth of detailed information which would serve only to obscure the diagnosis task.

4.2.2 Descriptive knowledge

The formulation of the heuristics used by an expert highlights concepts in the problem domain which are central to the problem-solving process. In effect, these concepts represent a distilled version of the expert's background knowledge without which it would not be possible to express the problem-solving heuristics. This knowledge is often termed *descriptive* knowledge. It provides a description of the problem domain at a level of abstraction which suppresses irrelevant detail but which makes explicit those features and characteristics which are important in the problem-solving process.

The problem-solving knowledge captured within an expert system is therefore a combination of heuristic and descriptive knowledge. The heuristic knowledge captures the active problem-solving strategies employed by the expert. However, it cannot be considered in isolation from the descriptive knowledge, since it would not be possible to express the heuristics without this supportive background knowledge.

4.3 CONCEPTUALIZATION AND FORMALIZATION OF KNOWLEDGE

When an expert is asked how he solves a problem, he describes his knowledge and problem-solving techniques using a natural language, such as English. Although this is a natural means of communication between human beings, it is not a suitable medium for communicating expertise to a computer program. The expert is likely to describe his expertise in terms such as:

If situation X occurs, then I do Y.

The key to expert system development is in allowing a computer program to recognize that situation 'X' has occurred. It is the role of the knowledge representation task in expert system building to ensure that this recognition of situations is in fact achieved. Therefore knowledge representation can be considered as the process of transferring the description of situations from the natural language domain to a descriptive framework which can be interpreted by computer programs.

During the expert system-building process, this transfer is achieved in two distinct phases:

(1)   Conceptualization
(2)   Formalization.

During the conceptualization phase, an initial study of the problem is carried out. The purpose of this study is to define the goal of the expert system and to identify the key concepts and relationships which form the basis for an expert's decisions.

The formalization phase consists of expressing these concepts and relationships in a formal framework supplied by an expert system-building tool.

4.3.1 Conceptualization

The conceptualization phase represents the first shift of domain knowledge out of the domain of natural language. During this phase, the important features of the problem domain must be characterized and the information which is directly relevant to the problem-solving process must be identified, i.e. the descriptive knowledge required in the problem-solving process. Owing to the richness of natural language, a large amount of information can be contained implicitly in a relatively small description. Much of this information can be discarded since it has no direct bearing on the problem solution. However, key parts of the information must be retained and, moreover, must be made explicit.

To identify descriptive knowledge, a knowledge engineer makes an initial study of the problem domain and then follows this up by observing an expert at work solving problems. The problem-solving knowledge must be expressed in terms of physical objects, abstract states, relationships, definitions and terminology which are used in the domain. All of these represent key concepts in the problem-solving process. These are the concepts which must be identified and described explicitly during the conceptualization phase. One of the harder tasks during this phase is to identify and extract the concepts which are implicit in the domain but which are an integral part of the problem-solving process.

During this phase also, the knowledge engineer must choose the level of detail at which the descriptive knowledge must be described. The appropriate level is usually the highest level of description (i.e. least detailed) at which the important concepts can be made explicit and which highlights the key information on which an expert's decisions are based.

To illustrate this process consider the conceptualization of the knowledge used by an expert mechanic when diagnosing engine-starting problems. At the first study of the domain, the key concepts might be identified as:

● battery
● starter

● timing
● etc.

However, this level of description does not make explicit the information
the expert uses when diagnosing a starting problem. Therefore further study
of the domain might result in the concepts being described at a greater level
of detail. This in turn introduces more concepts which were previously
implicit in the domain but which must now be made explicit. A more
detailed description might take the form:

battery
       status: charged
                           flat
starter
       status: normal
                           faulty
ignition circuit
       status: normal
                           faulty
spark plugs
       part-of: ignition circuit
       condition: normal
                           oily
                           sooty

The additional concepts introduced here include the status of the components, and values for the status which include 'charged', 'flat', 'normal'
and 'faulty'. The implicit knowledge that spark plugs are part of the ignition
circuit and that they may be in a normal, oily or sooty condition has also
been made explicit.

The conceptualization phase should result in a description of the problem
domain which effectively provides a vocabulary that allows the expert's
knowledge to be expressed with ease.

The explicit representation of the heuristic knowledge used by the expert
in the domain must always be preceded by the conceptualization phase.
The ease with which the expert's heuristics can be expressed using the
descriptive knowledge identified during this phase is a good indicator of
how complete the conceptualization has been. If heuristics can be expressed
without difficulty, this indicates that an appropriate level of description has
been achieved and the key concepts have been made explicit. If, however,
it is consistently difficult to express the expert's heuristics in terms of the
identified concepts, this indicates that an appropriate level of description
has not been found and that key concepts may still be missing.

4.3.2 Formalization

During the conceptualization phase, information from the problem domain
is reduced to a minimal set of concepts and relationships, sufficient to

formulate a semi-formal representation of the expert's rules. The formalization phase completes the transformation of this information into a representation which can be interpreted by a computer program. In general, this consists of expressing the concepts and relationships in a formal framework supplied by an expert system-building tool.

Every expert system-building tool is built around a framework for representing knowledge. The semi-formal (or structured) representation of the domain knowledge developed in the conceptualization phase must now be expressed using the framework provided by the expert system-building tool. If the expert system-building tool has already been selected, the objective of this phase is to find an appropriate mapping from the semi-formal domain knowledge into the formal representation mechanism provided by the tool. If the expert system-building tool has not yet been selected, the formalization phase can provide valuable input for the selection of the most appropriate tool for implementing the expert system.

A range of knowledge representation systems are available in expert system-building tools on the market today. The ease with which the knowledge from a particular problem domain fits into its representation framework is one of the criteria for judging the tool's suitability for implementing expert systems in that domain. If it is consistently difficult to express domain knowledge using the structures provided by the tool, it is likely that the tool is not ideally suited to the task.

Some of the more common knowledge representation mechanisms found in commercially available expert system-building tools will be described in later sections of this chapter. Irrespective of the knowledge representation mechanism used, however, tools must provide an integrated representation for both heuristic and descriptive knowledge.

4.4. REPRESENTING HEURISTIC KNOWLEDGE

Heuristic knowledge represents the strategic problem-solving knowledge applied by an expert. The expert may have a range of problem-solving techniques which he can apply in different situations or at different points of the problem-solving process. In general when solving a problem, the expert recognizes key patterns or features which allow him to decide the technique most likely to lead him towards an acceptable solution. A suitable representation mechanism for heuristic knowledge must capture this opportunistic character of the knowledge. One of the most common mechanisms which fulfils this objective is the production rule formalism.

4.4.1 Production rules
Production rules provide a natural formalism for representing heuristic knowledge. Production rules are generally represented in a form similar to IF–THEN statements. They are sometimes called 'situation–action' rules or 'antecedent–consequent' rules; e.g. the general form of a rule is:

IF <situation> THEN <action> or
IF <antecedent> THEN <consequent>

The <situation> or <antecedent> part of the rule is sometimes referred to as the *left-hand side* (LHS) and the <action> or <consequent> part of the rule is sometimes referred to as the *right-hand side* (RHS).

The left-hand side of a rule generally describes some situation or pattern of information in the problem domain. The right-hand side describes some action which it is recommended to take under the conditions described in the left-hand side, or some conclusion which is valid given the information in the left-hand side.

For example, to express the motor diagnosis heuristic shown above, we might write a simple rule such as:

        IF   (the engine does not start) AND
                  (the starter turns the engine normally) AND
                  (there is no spark at the spark plugs)
        THEN   (the ignition circuit is faulty)

In this example rule the RHS indicates a conclusion about the probable cause of the engine not starting, given the information about the engine contained in the LHS.

The left-hand side of a rule normally contains a number of clauses (surrounded by parentheses in this example) which are combined using logical connectives such as AND and OR. In addition, a NOT operator may be used to indicate that the rule should fire if the clause is not true. Thus the rule above might be rewritten with a NOT operator as shown below:

        IF   (the engine does not start) AND
                  (the starter turns the engine normally) AND
                  NOT (spark at the spark plugs)
        THEN   (the ignition circuit is faulty)

If all the condition clauses in a rule are found to be true, then the action or conclusion part of the rule can be activated. In this way, rules express valid inferences which can be made in the specific problem domain, i.e. if A is known to be true and if there is a rule which says 'If A then B', then it is valid to conclude that B is true.

There is no direct interaction between rules; rules cannot call or activate each other directly. The only mechanism for communication between rules is through the conclusions which can be inferred by a rule. When a rule has been successfully activated, it adds its conclusions to the set of facts which characterize the problem under consideration. These new facts may show the truth of some clauses in the LHS of rules, which were inactive up to this point. Those rules now become available for activation and their

conclusions can be used in turn to activate yet more rules. A small rule set
for motor diagnosis, consisting of three rules, is shown below:

Rule 1

IF (the engine does not start) AND
(the starter turns the engine normally) AND
NOT (spark at the spark plugs)

THEN (the ignition circuit is faulty)

Rule 2

IF (the ignition circuit is faulty) AND
(the contact breaker (CB) gap is normal) AND
(the battery is properly connected to the CB) AND
(the coil is properly connected to the CB) AND
(the resistance of the low-tension coil is normal)

THEN (the low-tension circuit is normal)

Rule 3

IF (the ignition circuit is faulty) AND
(the low-tension circuit is normal) AND
NOT (spark at the high-tension lead)

THEN (the coil is faulty)

In this example we can assume that we have generated the necessary facts
which allow Rule 1 to be activated. The effect of this is to generate a new
fact, i.e. that the ignition circuit is faulty. This new information now allows
Rule 2 to be activated, which in turn produces the information that the
low-tension circuit is normal. Now, armed with this fact, Rule 3 fires and
produces the conclusion that the coil is faulty.

In this way the independence of rules in relation to one another is assured.
Each rule only has to describe the particular situation in which it is activated.
As soon as this situation is encountered (either through information supplied
from outside or inferred by previous rule activations), the rule becomes
available for activation and the process can continue.

4.4.2 Certainty factors

In many problem domains the expert may use some form of judgemental
or inexact reasoning. For example, he may use heuristics such as 'When
conditions X and Y occur, Z *is likely* to be the cause' (although this may
not preclude other, though less likely, causes for the conditions). In some
cases the information used by the expert may be uncertain, i.e. he may
believe that a fact is true but may not be entirely certain. This type of
reasoning where some facts *suggest* others, and facts stated to be *probably*
true are manipulated, is common amongst human experts. To cope with
this kind of uncertainty, the simple fact and rule formalism is usually
extended to include a representation of the degree of certainty with which

a fact or conclusion can be considered to be true. This is usually represented as some number attached to a fact or rule and is often called a *certainty factor* (CF).

Certainty factors generally range from a minimum value, indicating that a fact is definitely false, to a maximum value, indicating that a fact is definitely true. Intermediate values indicate the strength with which a fact is believed. The actual range of values varies widely from system to system. One possibility is to allow certainty factors to range from 0 (definitely false) to 1 (definitely true). Another possibility is to use negative values to indicate the strength of disbelief in a fact while positive values indicate the strength of belief. Thus certainty factors in this case might range from −1 (definitely false) to +1 (definitely true).

We can modify Rule 1 above to incorporate certainty factors, thus representing the inexact reasoning which is used when diagnosing starting problems. In our example the defined range for certainty factors is from 0 to 1:

Rule 1
> IF   (the engine does not start) AND
>   (the starter turns the engine normally) AND
>   NOT (spark at the spark plugs)
>   THEN   (the ignition circuit is faulty (0.8))

In this example we have modified the rule to say that if the three conditions are true then we are reasonably certain (0.8) that the cause is a fault in the ignition circuit. Thus we have attached a CF of 0.8 to this rule. In this form the rule does not preclude the possibility (however remote) that some component other than the ignition circuit (the battery, say) may be at fault.

CFs attached to rules and facts interact with one another when a rule is activated. The facts which match the conditions in the LHS of a rule will have CFs associated with them. These certainty factors must be merged in some way with the CF associated with the rule. Although there is some resemblance between them, certainty factors are not the same as probabilities. In particular, certainty factors are usually combined in an empirical manner rather than by using the rigorous laws governing probabilities. A common formula for combining the CFs to calculate the CF for the new fact concluded by a rule is shown below:

$$CF<RHS> = CF<LHS> * CF<rule>$$

However, when a rule has multiple premises joined by AND or OR operators, how should we calculate the overall CF to be associated with the premise part of the rule? This problem is commonly solved by adopting the following convention:

● If the conditions are joined by an AND operator then the overall CF

for the LHS of the rule is taken to be the MINIMUM of the individual
CFs for the rule's conditions.
● If the conditions are joined by an OR operator then the overall CF for
the LHS of the rule is taken to be the MAXIMUM of the individual
CF's for the rule's conditions.

This simple convention has an intuitive appeal. If every condition on the
LHS of a rule must be true in order to activate the rule then it is reasonable
to say that our confidence in the LHS of the rule cannot exceed our
confidence in the weakest of those conditions. Put another way, we are
saying that a chain is only as strong as its weakest link. In contrast, if it is
sufficient that any condition of the LHS of a rule is true in order to activate
the rule then it is reasonable to say that our confidence in the LHS of the
rule need be no less than our confidence in the strongest condition.
   Now suppose that we are given the following facts:

● The engine does not start (1.0).
● The starter turns the engine normally (0.8).
● There is no spark at the spark plugs (1.0).

These facts state that we know for certain that the engine does not start
and that there is no spark at the spark plugs, while we only believe with a
certainty factor of 0.8 that the starter turns the engine over normally. With
these facts, Rule 1 can be activated and the certainty factors combined as
shown below:

$$CF <RHS> = MIN(1.0\ 0.8\ 1.0) * 0.8$$
$$= 0.8 * 0.8$$
$$= 0.64$$

Thus we can conclude with a certainty factor of 0.64 that there is a fault in
the ignition circuit.
   The use of certainty factors attached to facts and rules allows the
judgemental and inexact aspects of an expert's reasoning process to be
modelled. However, it is not an exact modelling process. The values assigned
to CFs and the techniques used to combine them are somewhat ad hoc and
can only be proven through the results that they produce.

4.5 REPRESENTING DESCRIPTIVE KNOWLEDGE

A number of techniques for representing descriptive knowledge have evolved over the years. The characteristics of the problem domain and of the
problem to be solved often indicate the selection of one technique over
another. In the next three subsections we will look at three common
knowledge representation mechanisms found in expert system development
environments.

4.5.1 The predicate calculus

In order to represent descriptive knowledge about some problem domain we must have a language which allows us to manipulate symbolic expressions. The predicate calculus is just such a language. In addition to allowing real world concepts and situations to be represented, the predicate calculus also provides a formal logic framework in which new data may be inferred from known facts by activating inference rules.

Facts are represented in the predicate calculus in the form of *formulae*. A formula is made up of a *predicate* and some arbitrary number of *arguments*. Formulae may be written in many different forms but a common notation found in many systems is shown below:

(PREDICATE arg1 arg2 . . . argN)

A formula is written as a list of symbols within parentheses. The first symbol represents the predicate and all remaining symbols denote arguments for the predicate. This is known as prefix notation.

In the predicate calculus a formula is either TRUE or FALSE and this forms the basis on which logical inferences can be made. For example, to describe a fact such as

BLOCK 2 is red

we might write the formula

(COLOUR BLOCK2 RED)

where COLOUR is a predicate and BLOCK2 and RED are arguments. If this formula is TRUE, this indicates that we believe that BLOCK2 is in fact red. If the formula is FALSE, we do not believe the fact represented by the formula.

The meaning attached to a formula is decided by the writer of the formula. Predicates may take any number of arguments and these arguments can be listed in any order. The representational power of the predicate calculus is derived from the freedom to introduce as many predicates into the calculus as are required. If meaningful names are chosen for the predicates then it is possible to 'read' the facts represented by formulae in the calculus so long as the convention adopted by the writer is known. Thus, for example, it would be equally valid to represent the fact that BLOCK2 is red by an alternative formula such as:

(RED BLOCK2)

Connectives are introduced into the predicate calculus so that simple formulae may be combined into more complex ones. The usual logical connectives are generally used: AND, OR and NOT. It is possible to represent facts such as

BLOCK2 is either red or blue
BLOCK2 and BLOCK3 are on TABLE1
BLOCK3 is not green

by using logical connectives as shown below:

    (OR (COLOUR BLOCK2 RED) (COLOUR BLOCK2 BLUE))
    (AND (ON BLOCK2 TABLE1) (ON BLOCK3 TABLE1))
    (NOT (COLOUR BLOCK3 GREEN))

4.5.1.1 Variables and quantifiers

In the examples shown above we have used the predicate calculus to describe simple facts. However, much of the information in the real world consists of more general knowledge than mere descriptive facts. For example, we could use the formulae

    (ISA CLYDE ELEPHANT)
    (COLOUR CLYDE GREY)

to say that 'Clyde is an elephant' and 'Clyde is grey', but how would we represent general knowledge such as 'All elephants are grey'?

The power of the predicate calculus to represent this kind of general information comes from the introduction of variables and quantifiers into the language.

As in a mathematical language, variables in the predicate calculus are used as placeholders for objects or concepts in the world described by the calculus. The purpose of the quantifiers is to determine how the variable is to be interpreted.

There are two types of quantifiers defined in the predicate calculus: *existential quantifiers* and *universal quantifiers*. Universal quantifiers say that something is true for all possible values of a variable. Existential quantifiers say that something is true for some values of a variable. In this chapter we use FORALL as a universal quantifier and EXISTS as an existential quantifier.

Now we can express the fact that

    All elephants are grey

by the following formula which contains a variable and a universal quantifier:

    (FORALL (X) (IF (ISA X ELEPHANT) (COLOUR X GREY))

This formula states that for all objects, if it is true that the object is an elephant, then the colour of the object is grey.

Using an existential quantifier and a variable we can express the fact that

Some cats have no tails

by the formula:

(EXISTS (X) (AND (ISA X CAT) (NOT (HAS X TAIL))))

This formula states that for some object X, if it is true that the object is a cat, then it is true that the object does not have a tail.

Note that in these quantified expressions, if there is any object for which the expression is true, the variable X is said to be *bound* to that object.

It is possible to embed one quantified expression inside another one and so express even more complex situations. For example, to say that every ship has a captain we might use the formula:

```
(FORALL (X) (IF              (ISA X SHIP)
       (EXISTS (Y) (AND      (ISA Y PERSON)
                            (ON-BOARD Y X)
                            (STATUS Y CAPTAIN)))))
```

This formula states that for every object X that is a ship, there is some person Y who is on board the ship and whose status is captain of the ship.

4.5.1.2 Deducing new facts

The predicate calculus provides a formal basis for making logical deductions from known facts. If all the formulae describing a world are placed in a database, then the database represents all the facts which we currently believe to be true in that world, i.e. this represents a knowledge base. Now if we have a set of rules describing the logical implications which are defined in that world, then by applying those rules over the formulae in the knowledge base we are able to augment the knowledge base with new facts deduced from the original formulae. For example, from the information that Clyde is an elephant, and knowing that all elephants are grey, it is possible for us to deduce the new fact that Clyde is grey.

The general form of a logical implication in the predicate calculus is:

(IF p THEN q)

This formula states that if we are given *p*, and the logical implication (IF p THEN q) is true, then we can infer *q*. This type of inference is often referred to as *modus ponens*.

As an illustration of logical deduction we will show how the new fact 'Clyde is grey' is deduced. Assume that our database contains the two formulae shown below:

(1)   (ISA CLYDE ELEPHANT)
      'Clyde is an elephant'
(2)   (FORALL (X)   (IF   (ISA X ELEPHANT)
                       THEN   (COLOUR X GREY)))
      'All elephants are grey'

Note that a logical implication is used to represent the fact that all elephants are grey.

Now matching (1) against (2) we can see that the variable X can be bound to CLYDE. Therefore we can generate a logical implication using this binding as shown below:

(3)   (IF (ISA CLYDE ELEPHANT
      THEN (COLOUR CLYDE GREY))
      'If Clyde is an elephant then Clyde is grey'

Now using *modus ponens* on this implication we can deduce a new fact as shown below:

(4)   (COLOUR CLYDE GREY)
      'Clyde is grey'

4.5.1.3 Motor diagnosis example

The framework provided by the predicate calculus for representing descriptive knowledge is easily integrated with the rule formalism required to represent the heuristics expressed by Rules 1–3 described earlier.

The first step is to define the set of predicates which will be used to describe the problem domain. From an examination of the heuristics, a minimal set of predicates as shown below are required:

  (STATUS *component value*)
  (PART-OF *component system*)
  (CONDITION *component value*)
  (CONNECTED *component component*)
  (SPARK *component value*)
  (RESISTANCE *component value*)

The STATUS predicate allows us to describe the status of a component, e.g.

  (STATUS battery charged)

states that the battery is charged. The other predicates are used in a similar fashion.

Now, on the basis of these predicates we can rewrite the rules in a formalized manner as shown below:

Rule 1
```
    (IF        (AND      (STATUS engine does-not-start)
                         (STATUS starter normal)
                         (NOT (SPARK spark-plug normal)))
    THEN
               (STATUS ignition-circuit faulty))
```

Rule 2
```
    (IF        (AND      (STATUS ignition-circuit faulty)
                         (STATUS CB-gap normal)
                         (CONNECTED battery CB)
                         (CONNECTED LT-coil CB)
                         (RESISTANCE LT-coil normal))
    THEN
               (STATUS LT-circuit normal))
```

Rule 3
```
    (IF        (AND      (STATUS ignition-circuit faulty)
                         (STATUS LT-circuit normal)
                         (NOT (SPARK HT-lead normal))
    THEN
               (STATUS coil faulty))
```

The predicate calculus provides a powerful and flexible representation for knowledge. In addition it provides a sound framework for making logical deductions, inferring new facts from known facts. However, it is largely an unstructured form of representation, i.e. formulae are entered into a database in random order. Whenever we are looking for information about Clyde, say, there is no guarantee that the formulae describing Clyde will be adjacent to one another in the knowledge base. Locating all the facts about Clyde might entail searching the whole knowledge base from top to bottom. This leads to very inefficient retrieval of information from the knowledge base. A structured representation of knowledge helps to overcome this problem by ensuring that facts relating to a single object or concept are grouped together by some means. Semantic networks and frames both provide a structured representation of knowledge.

4.5.2 Semantic networks

In contrast to the predicate calculus, semantic networks provide a structured representation for knowledge. In a semantic network the information described by a predicate calculus formula may be described by means of nodes and directed arcs as shown in Fig. 4.1:

```
    (ISA CLYDE ELEPHANT)
    (COLOUR CLYDE GREY)
```

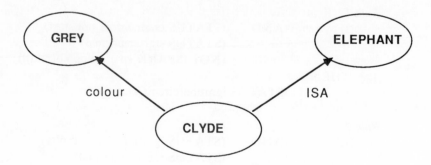

Fig. 4.1 — A sematic network.

In this description the nodes represent the objects, concepts or events in the world being described. The names on the arcs correspond to names of relations and the arcs indicate which concepts or objects are linked by the relations. As more information is represented, new nodes and arcs are added, some of which may be linked to nodes already in the network. In this way a large and, potentially, highly interconnected network can be built up. As in the case of the predicate calculus, semantic networks are a very flexible form of representation. New nodes and arcs are added as they are needed and the network builder decides what meaning should be to attached them.

In addition, the structure of the network provides a form of indexing of information in the knowledge base. To retrieve everything we know about Clyde, we simply follow all the arcs which lead from the Clyde node in the network. However, this indexing of information is not the only significant advantage to be gained by this form of representation; it can also provide a mechanism for *inheritance*.

4.5.2.1 Inheritance
We know that if Clyde is an elephant then he must be grey. In the predicate calculus we can represent this type of information indirectly by defining the appropriate logical implication. Then, given the fact that Clyde is an elephant, we can deduce that Clyde is grey. However, the same information can be represented directly in the structure of a semantic network by means of inheritance.

Inheritance refers to the ability of one node to inherit characteristics from other nodes in the network. This is achieved through defining a special arc, usually called ISA ('is a'). A special property of the ISA arc is that properties can be transmitted from one node to another along it.

To represent the information that 'All elephants are grey' in a semantic network, we simply add an Elephant node to the network and attach a COLOUR arc pointing to the value GREY. Now, by linking the Clyde node to the Elephant node by an ISA arc as shown, we allow Clyde to inherit all the characteristics of elephants. Thus, when we look for the

COLOUR property of Clyde, the COLOUR property from the Elephant node is transmitted to Clyde, and we know that Clyde is grey.

However, inheritance does not have to be limited to a single ISA arc. Some of the information that we know about elephants is due to the fact that they share characteristics which are common to all mammals, and mammals in turn share characteristics which are common to living organisms, etc. Therefore we can build up an ISA hierarchy as shown in Fig. 4.2. Now Clyde inherits properties not only from elephants, but also from mammals and living organisms as well.

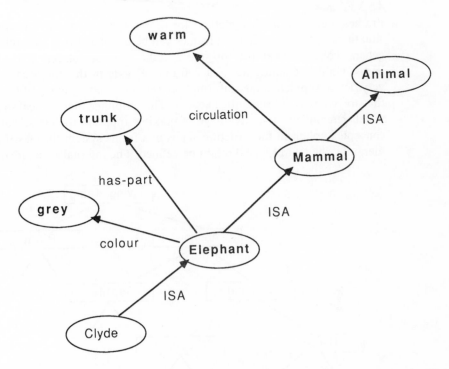

Fig. 4.2 — An ISA hierarchy.

Using the inheritance mechanism, it is possible to represent knowledge in well-structured classification hierarchies, or taxonomies. The ISA relation can represent class/subclass relationships as in the link between mammal and elephant. It can also represent class/member relationships such as between elephant and Clyde. Nodes lower down the hierarchy inherit properties from nodes higher in the classification. This is an efficient form of representation since information common to many nodes need only be represented explicitly in one single location. Information in the knowledge base is accessed by following the appropriate arcs from the object of interest. The task of maintaining the knowledge base is also simplified since information need only be added or deleted in a single location.

A disadvantage of semantic networks is that they rely to a large extent on a graphical notation of nodes and arcs. Although this notation is easily interpreted by humans, it is unwieldy when translated into a form which can be processed by a computer. For this reason semantic networks have not been widely adopted in computer implementations of knowledge representation systems. Frame-based systems, however, lend themselves to efficient computer implementations and share many of the interesting characteristics of semantic networks. In the next subsection we will examine the use of frames as a means for the representation of knowledge.

4.5.3 Frames

Frames represent another method for representing common concepts and situations. Like semantic nets, frames can be organized in a hierarchy with general concepts near the top and specific concepts placed at the lower levels. Unlike semantic nets, each frame or node in this hierarchy can be very rich in supplementary information, thus eliminating many of the nodes that are required in a semantic network. The simplified hierarchical structure which remains has the advantage of making apparent the classification of concepts implicit in the structure. Thus in a frame system the classification hierarchy shown in Fig. 4.3 might be defined. The internal structure of each

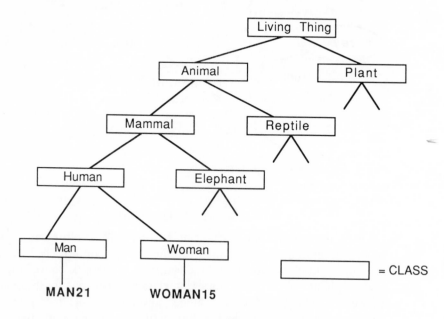

Fig. 4.3 — A Frame Hierarchy.

frame occurring in the hierarchy can be quite complex. In general, a frame is structured much as an object with a collection of attributes. For example, the frame describing John Smith may be structured as shown in Fig. 4.4. Note the use of VALUE: associated with each of the attribute names. This indicates that the information which follows it is to be interpreted as the value of the attribute. Therefore we can see that the MAN21 frame

MAN21

IS-A	VALUE:	MAN
Name	VALUE:	John Smith
Height	VALUE:	1.90
Weight	VALUE:	95
Hobbies	VALUE:	Jogging, Tennis

Fig. 4.4 — Frame describing John Smith

represents a man whose name is John Smith and whose height, weight and hobbies are as described.

In frame terminology a frame is made up of four levels of description: *frame, slot, facet* and *data*. The name of the frame is the only information represented at the *frame* level. The attributes of the frame are normally represented at the *slot* level. The *facet* level indicates different aspects of an attribute for which information may be stored in the frame. The *data* level is the lowest level in the frame and information about the attributes is stored at this level.

As shown above, slots can be used to represent attributes or properties of a frame. However, slots can also be used to represent relationships between frames. When the value of the slot indicates the name of another frame, the name of the slot can be considered to be the name of a relationship between the frames. This is the meaning of the IS-A slot in the example frame above; it establishes the IS-A link between MAN21 and the more general MAN frame.

4.5.3.1 Passive facets

The use of a supplementary level of description, the facet, between the slot and data levels is a very important feature of frames and is responsible for much of the flexibility of representation for which frames are noted. In the example above, the facet level is used to indicate the value of an attribute or slot. However, other aspects of a slot may also be of interest; for example, a default value to be used if no explicit value is specified, constraints on the type of data which can be placed in the slot, etc. Supplementary information like this can be specified by defining appropriate facets such as DEFAULT: and TYPE:. Examples of these facets are shown in the general MAN frame of Fig. 4.5. The average height and weight of a man

MAN

IS-A	VALUE:	MAMMAL
Height	TYPE:	Real
	DEFAULT:	1.80
Weight	TYPE:	Real
	DEFAULT:	65

Fig. 4.5 — General Frame Describing the Class of MAN

are now specified as default values for those slots. Now if we try to retrieve a value for John Smith's height or weight and no value is found in the appropriate slots of the MAN21 frame, the default values specified in the MAN frame can be returned in their place. In this way, one interpretation of the default values is to assert that, unless we are told specifically otherwise, we may assume that John Smith is a man of average height and weight.

The frame system itself is normally responsible for making use of this type of information. For example, the data retrieval procedure may be implemented in such a way that if a value is not retrieved from a VALUE: facet in a slot, it will automatically look for inherited values further up the class hierarchy. Then, if this fails, it may look for a default value, either local or inherited.

Slots may be used to build user-defined relationships between frames. For example, we could define a Married-to slot in the MAN21 frame whose value would indicate the frame representing John Smith's wife. By means of this relationship it is possible to retrieve information about John Smith's wife by accessing the appropriate frame.

4.5.3.2 Active facets

So far we have seen that data in a frame may be used to represent some descriptive information about a slot. The facets which store this type of information are called passive facets because they are used to store information which may subsequently be retrieved from the frame. However, facets in a frame may also have an active nature. The information in these facets represents procedural attachments (arbitrary programmes) which are executed whenever the value of a slot is changed. Typical active facets found in frame systems are:

IF-ADDED	Activated whenever a new value is placed in the slot
IF-REMOVED:	Activated whenever a value is deleted from the slot
IF-NEEDED:	Activated when the value of a slot is required but no value has yet been inserted in the slot

Procedures attached to slots in this manner can be used to describe actions which should be executed whenever the slot values are changed in some way. To illustrate how these procedures might be used in a frame system, consider the updated frame representing John Smith in Fig. 4.6.

Procedural attachments have been used to maintain consistency within the Married-to relationship; i.e. if John is married to Mary then the IF-ADDED: procedure ensures that we can retrieve the information that Mary is married to John. Similarly, if we remove the information that John is married to Mary then the IF-REMOVED: procedure ensures that John is removed from the Married-to slot in the frame representing Mary. An IF-NEEDED: attachment has been used to establish that if John and Mary

MAN21

IS-A	VALUE:	MAN
Name	VALUE:	John Smith
Height	VALUE:	
Weight	VALUE:	
Hobbies	VALUE:	Jogging, Tennis
Married-to	VALUE:	WOMAN15
	IF-ADDED:	(Add MAN21 to the Married-to slot of WOMAN15)
	IF-REMOVED:	(Delete MAN21 from the Married-to slot of WOMAN15)
Children	IF-NEEDED:	(Find the value of the Children slot in WOMAN15)

Fig. 4.6 — Detailed Frame Describing John Smith

are married then we can find out the names of John's children by looking at the names of Mary's children.

Procedural attachments cannot be executed directly but are activated automatically by the frame system whenever the specified operations are carried out on slot values. For this reason, procedural attachments are sometimes referred to as *demons*. This facility for combining procedural knowledge with declarative knowledge in a single representation framework is a powerful feature of frame systems. There are many situations in which knowledge is quite naturally represented in a procedural manner and frame systems provide the knowledge engineer with an appropriate medium to avoid unnatural declarative representations for this kind of knowledge.

The powerful features provided by a frame representation provide a useful base on which to build an expert system. The descriptive knowledge can be properly structured and represented within the frame hierarchy. Heuristic knowledge is added to the system by adding rules which are designed to match the slot values for specified frames. In addition, procedural attachments may be used to extend the information-gathering facilities of the expert system. For example, IF-NEEDED: procedures may be defined to query the user or an external database whenever some required information is not available in the frame hierarchy.

4.5.3.3 Motor diagnosis example
Heuristic knowledge and descriptive knowledge are easily integrated into a representation framework based on frames. Some of the frames which would be used to represent the descriptive knowledge for the motor diagnosis example are shown in Fig. 4.7. Two general frames are defined: COMPONENT and COMPLEX-COMPONENT. These are the most general concepts occurring in the problem domain. All the components of an engine (including the engine itself) can be classified in terms of one of these two classes. The slots belonging to these frames are inherited by the frames

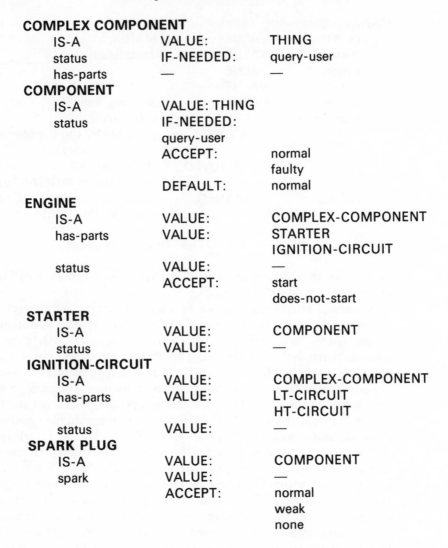

COMPLEX COMPONENT
IS-A	VALUE:	THING
status	IF-NEEDED:	query-user
has-parts	—	—

COMPONENT
IS-A	VALUE: THING	
status	IF-NEEDED: query-user	
	ACCEPT:	normal
		faulty
	DEFAULT:	normal

ENGINE
IS-A	VALUE:	COMPLEX-COMPONENT
has-parts	VALUE:	STARTER
		IGNITION-CIRCUIT
status	VALUE:	—
	ACCEPT:	start
		does-not-start

STARTER
IS-A	VALUE:	COMPONENT
status	VALUE:	—

IGNITION-CIRCUIT
IS-A	VALUE:	COMPLEX-COMPONENT
has-parts	VALUE:	LT-CIRCUIT
		HT-CIRCUIT
status	VALUE:	—

SPARK PLUG
IS-A	VALUE:	COMPONENT
spark	VALUE:	—
	ACCEPT:	normal
		weak
		none

Fig. 4.7 — Frames for the Motor Example

representing actual components of the engine. The 'has-parts' slot of the
COMPLEX-COMPONENT frame indicates that a complex component is
made up of some combination of other components. The 'status' slot of
both frames serves the same purpose as the STATUS predicate in the
predicate calculus. However, in the COMPONENT frame it is possible to
augment the slot with two additional pieces of information: an IF-NEEDED
demon, which automatically asks the user to supply a value for the slot
when necessary; and an ACCEPTS: facet, which indicates the two acceptable values for the 'status' slot — 'normal' and 'faulty'.

The other frames represent instantiations of these two frames which
describe actual components found in an engine.

To integrate heuristic knowledge into this descriptive framework, rules
can be written in terms of *frame*, *slot* and *value* triplets. The example rules
shown above for motor diagnosis can be rewritten in terms of the frames
as shown below:

Rule 1

    (IF   (AND   (ENGINE status does-not-start)

                            (STARTER status normal)

                            (SPARK-PLUG spark normal))

    THEN

                (IGNITION-CIRCUIT status faulty))

Rule 2

    (IF   (AND   (IGNITION-CIRCUIT status faulty)

                            (CONTACT-BREAKER gap normal)

                            (CONTACT-BREAKER   battery-connection
normal)

                            (CONTACT-BREAKER   lt-coil-connection
normal)

                            (COIL lt-resistance normal))

    THEN

                (LT-CIRCUIT status normal))

Rule 3

    (IF   (AND   (IGNITION-CIRCUIT status faulty)

                            (LT-CIRCUIT status normal)

                            (HT-LEAD spark none))

    THEN

                (COIL status faulty))

4.6 CONCLUSION

In this chapter we have looked at two different types of knowledge which
are applied by experts during the problem-solving process: heuristic knowledge and descriptive knowledge. For a computer-based expert system to
deliver a performance equivalent to a human expert, it must be capable of
incorporating these two types of knowledge into its knowledge base.

Production rules have evolved as the most common representation for
heuristic knowledge. Heuristics represent individual 'chunks' of knowledge
retained by the expert. An individual rule represents a single chunk of
knowledge. There is no direct interaction between rules; rules cannot call
or activate each other. This independence leads to a certain modularity in
the knowledge base and, in theory, allows for an incremental development
of the knowledge base simply by adding new rules as required.

In practice, the rule-based formalism suffers from some disadvantages:

● It is not always possible to derive natural and readable rules which are also efficient to execute. Very often, some trade-off between these extremes is necessary.
● It is difficult to ensure independence between rules in a large knowledge base. As the number of rules grows, it is more and more likely that the rule set may contain contradictions or that general rules may subsume more specific ones. Thus adding new rules may have unpredictable effects on the behaviour of a system.

Some of these limitations can be overcome by decomposing a rule base into separate modules, each module containing rules which deal with only one aspect of the problem domain. If only one module is active at a time, interactions between rules can be minimized and system performance can be improved owing to the reduced number of rules to be scanned in each inference cycle.

A number of different mechanisms for representing descriptive knowledge have been discussed. The predicate calculus provides a powerful and flexible representation for this type of knowledge. It also provides a sound framework for making logical deductions. However, it is largely an unstructured representation. This problem can be partially overcome by adding an indexing facility to the predicate logic knowledge base.

Semantic networks and frames, in contrast, provide structured representation of descriptive knowledge. In addition, the concept of inheritance considerably reduces redundant information in the knowledge base and effectively eases the problem of maintaining the knowledge base.

A disadvantage of semantic networks, however, is that they rely to a large extent on a graphical notation of nodes and arcs which is unwieldy when translated into computer data structures. Frame-based systems, however, lend themselves to efficient computer implementations and provide a unified framework for declarative and procedural representation of knowledge. For these reasons, frames are the most common representation for descriptive knowledge in the large hybrid toolsets such as KEE or ART, and are to be found increasingly in the advanced expert system tools now available on powerful personal computers.

REFERENCES

Charniak, E., & McDermott, D. (1985) *Introduction to artificial intelligence.* Addison-Wesley, Reading, MA
Harmon, P., & King, D. (1985) *Expert systems.* Wiley, New York
Hayes-Roth, F., Waterman, D., & Lenat, B. (1983). *Building expert systems.* Addison-Wesley, Reading, MA
Silverman, B. G. (ed.) (1987) *Expert systems for business.* Addison-Wesley, Reading, MA
Waterman, D. (1986) *A guide to expert systems.* Addison-Wesley, Reading MA

Weiss, S., & Kulikowski, C. (1984) *A practical guide to designing expert systems*. Rowman & Allanheld Totowa, NJ

Winston, P. H. (1984) *Artificial intelligence*. 2nd ed. Addison-Wesley, Reading, MA

5

Tools for building expert systems

Khalid P. Ishaq

5.1 INTRODUCTION

One of the major tasks of the knowledge engineer is to determine what tool to use when building an expert system. This is a very important stage in the construction of an expert system; indeed the success or failure of the expert system may depend on choosing the right tool. Thus the knowledge engineer must be aware of what facilities he demands in a tool. This can only be achieved through an investigation of the domain and an analysis of the user requirements. This chapter assumes that the knowledge engineer has completed these phases and is at the stage where he is selecting a tool to build the expert system. To this end this chapter considers the various factors the knowledge engineer should consider when selecting a tool to build an expert system. The chapter will provide an explanation of why each facility may be required in the tool and the important characteristics of that facility. We shall state for each facility the extent to which it is implemented or can be implemented in the various expert system tools. We shall also try to outline some guidelines to follow for each facility. However, before this we shall provide a brief overview of expert system tools.

The aim of this chapter is not to list the pros and cons of various expert system tools but to look at the major factors the knowledge engineer should consider when selecting a tool to build an expert system. Although specific reference will be made to the facilities provided by some shells/languages, the name of the product will not be mentioned.

5.2 EXPERT SYSTEM TOOLS

At present, expert system-building tools fall into three main categories.

(1) *Languages*. These are of two types: firstly, languages specifically designed for expert system development, such as Prolog and Lisp, which will be referred to as artificial intelligence (AI) languages; secondly, conventional languages such as C or Pascal. However, this is not to say that expert systems cannot be written in conventional languages, although Prolog and Lisp provide more facilities for building expert systems. Some of these facilities include:

- Symbolic representation — words can be represented in Prolog and Lisp using atoms. This makes it very convenient to represent knowledge, although this can be implemented in a conventional language using a string.
- Debugging facilities — traces of the control flow of the program make it possible to quickly develop the expert system.
- Data structures to represent knowledge — manipulation of list structures in Lisp and Prolog makes it possible to quickly represent knowledge. In conventional languages pointers have to be used to manipulate the list structure, and this makes for a more cumbersome program.

Although Prolog and Lisp have more appropriate basic facilities for building expert systems than conventional languages, there may also be other factors to consider when selecting a language to build an expert system. For example, the speed of the expert system may be a crucial factor. Prolog and Lisp are interpreted languages and although compilers have been developed for these languages they are still found to be slower in execution than conventional languages. Another factor to consider is interfaces to databases and other external programs (see sections 5.8 and 5.9). For example, would it be easier to integrate a graphics package to C than to Prolog or Lisp?

(2) *Expert system shells.* These provide the knowledge engineer with the inference engine, user interface and knowledge representation scheme to build expert systems. Once the knowledge engineer has coded the knowledge into the representation scheme, he has completed the expert system. Commercial examples include Crystal, Xi plus and ESP Advisor.

(3) *Knowledge-engineering tools.* These are large and complex expert system shells with various representation schemes and inferencing strategies (shells are usually limited to one knowledge representation scheme and inferencing method). Knowledge-engineering tools are large memory-intensive programs that require dedicated workstations. Commercial examples include KEE, ART and Knowledge Craft.

Although in theory expert systems can be implemented in any of the above three categories of tools, in practice it is not possible to deliver usable expert systems in knowledge-engineering tools since they are normally implemented on large-scale workstation environments. The facilities provided by knowledge-engineering tools are specifically aimed at helping knowledge engineers develop prototype systems. However, once the prototype is completed it will have to be delivered using an expert system shell or a language. This chapter will concentrate on expert system shells and languages for the reasons of practicality mentioned above.

5.3 KNOWLEDGE REPRESENTATION

The knowledge representation method selected for the domain will have a significant impact on the tool the knowledge engineer chooses to build the expert system. Buchanan & Shortliffe (1984) define representing knowledge as a:

> ... means of choosing a set of conventions for describing objects, relations and processes in the world. One first chooses a conceptual framework for thinking about the world — symbolically or numerically, centered around objects or processes and so forth. Then one needs to choose conventions within a given computer language for implementing the concepts.

Experience suggests that the way in which knowledge is represented within an expert system will have a significant impact upon the ease with which a particular development can be conducted. Certain application areas (or domains) seem to naturally suggest a particular representation method. The importance of representation in the overall success of the expert system cannot be underestimated. However, the knowledge engineer must be able to identify the appropriate knowledge representation method from the characteristics of the domain. Consequently, a major task is to establish the nature of the relationships between domain features and knowledge representation formalisms. A natural precondition for this requirement is a clear understanding of the range of possibilities in knowledge representation and the strengths and weaknesses of each one (for further details, see Chapter 4).

The aim of this section is not to consider what representation methodology the knowledge engineer should choose, but what tool he should select once he has chosen the representation methodology. For a discussion of what criteria to use when selecting a knowledge representation method see Ramsey *et al.* (1986).

We shall examine the two main methods of representing knowledge in expert systems — the production rule and the frame system. Although we shall not specifically mention semantic networks, our comments about frame systems also apply to semantic networks. In any case if we add defaults and procedural attachment to semantic networks, they are equivalent to frame systems; this was in fact done in KL-ONE (Brachman and Schmolze 1979).

5.3.1 Production rules

Production rules are conditional statements of the IF–THEN type, with a condition and an associated action. For example:

```
IF      X has a blocked nose and
        X has a sore throat and
        X has watery eyes
THEN    X has a cold
```

A rule is said to be triggered if the condition part is satisfied and the operations specified by the action part are performed. Thus if X has a blocked nose, a sore throat and watery eyes then we can conclude that X has a cold. Rules are of a modular form and are operated singly to make a specific change to the working memory, which will lead to the triggering of further rules, allowing the generation of a decision tree.

A large number of expert system shells only have one method of representing knowledge, i.e. the production rule. This tends to be fine in domains where the knowledge can be represented using IF . . . THEN conditionals. If the knowledge engineer can represent the knowledge using production rules then he has at his disposal a variety of tools to select from. However, for many applications this has proved to be a limited method of representing knowledge. In many domains the knowledge cannot be represented using production rules since the knowledge cannot be structured using IF . . . THEN statements. For example, in the project management domain there is often no right or wrong answer to a problem; often managers do not themselves know how they make decisions.

In structured domains there is usually only one solution to a problem — e.g. the prevalence of certain symptoms will lead a doctor to a certain conclusion and a possible remedy. In these domains the remedy is tried and tested and in most cases will bring about the desired result. In more complex domains even successful solutions applied in the past may not succeed today. This is because the environment outside the control of the decision maker is susceptible to change — e.g. in the project management domain the fluctuation of interest rates makes it difficult to make decisions. In structured domains the environment remains constant.

The knowledge engineer should be aware that most expert system shells do not have any way of structuring the production rules. Where it can be done, it is commonly achieved through the use of meta-rules. These are rules that control the inferencing strategy and are in practice used to fine-tune the knowledge base by controlling the firing of particular rules or rule groups. Meta-rules can cut down the search space in the domain, which is especially desirable in unstructured domains where the total number of rules is quite large and, hence, there is a need to explicitly declare what rules are applicable under what conditions (Ishaq & Beaumont 1988).

If using a conventional programming language the knowledge engineer would be required to implement the production rule representation. In AI languages the definition of a representation scheme is not a great problem. For example, in Prolog the rules could be represented using Horn clauses and the Internal Prolog interpreter used to control the rule firing. They could also be represented as Prolog assertions and an interpreter built to fire these rules. This approach provides the flexibility of adding meta-rules. The main problems involved in implementing the production rule in a language are the problems that will be encountered in building the inference strategies which control the rules (see section 5.4 on inferencing strategies).

5.3.2 Frame systems
A frame is a data structure for representing a stereotyped situation. Attached to each frame are several kinds of information which indicate how to use the frame, what one can expect to happen next or what to do if expectations

are not confirmed. Each frame may have a number of slots which refer to the properties named by the frame. For example, the frame for a *'Person'* might have slots for their *'Name'*, *'Height'*, *'Weight'* and so on. Each of these slots will have a value (filler) attached to it. For example, the *'Name'* of the *'Person'* may be Fred, his *'Height'* may be 1.8 m and so on. A slot will have several types of values, including:

● a constrained value, e.g. the slot *'age'* would be constrained by an integer between 0 and 120.
● a default value, e.g. unless there is contrary evidence assume that all people like flowers.

To represent a particular person, the frame user will create an instance of the *'Person'* frame and fill in the slots with the relevant information, e.g. *'Name'* may be assigned the value *'Fred Bloggs'*. Frames are organized into a hierarchy which allows the transfer of values through the process of inheritance. For example, if the *'Person'* frame were represented as a *'Mammal'* then it would inherit all the properties in the *'Mammal'* frame, such as the *'Mammal'* is *'warm blooded'*. This provides an efficient method of storing information because one does not have to store with each *'Person'* the fact that it is *'warm blooded'*; it can be stored in the *'Mammal'* frame.

Slots can be assigned values in a number of ways. The first two methods, *inheritance* and *default values*, are inexpensive ones and do not require a very powerful reasoning process. The third method, *procedural attachment* requires some computation; this method represents knowledge procedurally by assigning routines (procedures) to specific slots. These routines are activated whenever a value of a slot is changed or derived. They implement forward chaining control when certain events occur (demons) — e.g. a demon can be used to modify a person's bank account once the event 'received wages' has occurred for the individual.

Analysis of the data may reveal that the knowledge should be represented using a frame architecture. Many earlier expert system shells do not incorporate this formalism, although shells produced recently have introduced this method of representing knowledge.

Although expert systems may provide the general framework of a frame system, there may still be facilities required in the expert system that cannot be built into the expert system shell, e.g. the concept of multiple inheritance whereby a frame can inherit properties from more than one frame. In knowledge-engineering tools, control structures can be added to those that have already been built into the system. This provides the flexibility of catering for most types of situations.

Building a representation scheme in a programming language to implement a frame system can be achieved with little difficulty. For example, in Prolog it would merely amount to an assertion with fields for the various slots, instances and hierarchy representation. In a conventional language such as Pascal it could be represented as a record with pointers defining where it belongs in the frame hierarchy. The complexity lies in developing the control strategies that manipulate the frame hierarchy. This may take some time and effort, and the knowledge engineer should be aware of this before embarking on such a task (see section 5.4 on inferencing strategies).

5.3.3 Internal representation of knowledge

When we consider selecting a tool to build an expert system, the knowledge representation issue is concerned not only with the method of expressing the knowledge but also how the tool internally stores the knowledge. This will be by using variables, but how the variables are created within the tool is an important factor.

Most tools tend to have the general variable types such as:

    integer
    string
    real
    boolean

However, there may also be a need to describe knowledge using a group of related objects, where the group has a set of common characteristics and each object in the group has its own unique value for each of the characteristics. For example, suppose that one was building a real estate expert system: then part of the knowledge base would consist of real estate properties. As a group the properties will have common characteristics such as address, number of bedrooms, price and so forth. Individually each property has its own value for each of these characteristics. In most expert system shells this knowledge would have to be expressed with a number of global attributes, one for each characteristic of each real estate property — e.g. if there were 100 properties with 10 characteristics each, one would have to declare 1000 global variables. In some expert system shells this can be represented using class variables. For example:

    house:
    price:integer
    no-of-bedrooms:integer
    garage:boolean
    address:string
    central-heating:boolean
    area:string
    end

Then other variables can be declared of this type. For example,

    house1,house2:house

defines two variables house1 and house2, each of which have the characteristics of the house definition.

In expert system shells where there are no class variables this can lead to a number of problems. Firstly, it makes it difficult to structure the program since there are so many global variables. The effects of this are to make the program difficult to test and debug (see section 5.7 on debugging). Secondly, it can also lead to proliferation of the program code since the same procedures may have to be written using variables with the same meaning but with a different instantiation. For example, in the real estate expert system there may have to be a different rule for the price of house1 and the price of house2; with class variables a general rule would be defined for all the prices of houses. Without class variables the size of the program is increased, making it possible to implement only small expert systems in these shells.

Class variables can be defined in conventional programming languages, e.g. they could be defined as a C structure or a Pascal record. Also, they can quite easily be defined in AI languages such as Prolog or Lisp. In Prolog each house could be defined as a separate assertion — there would be no definition of the variables; the assertions would simply contain the relevant information or, if this was not available, there may be an uninstantiated variable. For example,

house('26 Montague Road',35000,no,yes,north)

represents a house at the address 26 Montague Road, priced at 35000, with no central heating, a garage and is situated in the north region of the district. In Prolog the relative position of the argument defines its intended meaning, e.g. the third argument indicates whether the house has central heating.

5.3.4 Variable instantiation
How the variables are assigned values in the tool is another important factor one should consider. The traditional method is by the expert system posing the user a question. This is available in all expert system shells and can easily be implemented in any programming language. However, there will be occasions in some applications where this is not sufficient. The following methods may also be required:

(1) Assignment within the tool — this is where the knowledge engineer can assign a value to a variable within the tool. For example, the knowledge engineer may want to re-ask a specific question. Once the question has already been asked, the question variable will be assigned a particular value; the knowledge engineer can re-ask the question by assigning to the question variable a value status of *not-yet-asked*. In some shells this process can be used to provide a looping mechanism. Clearly this problem does not arise in a programming language, where the knowledge engineer has greater control of the process.

(2) An external file — the file will contain information that the expert system requires to make conclusions. The expert system will gather the

information from the file rather than ask the user. In some domains it may be quicker to get information into the expert system via an external medium ˆrather than from the user, e.g. fault diagnosis of circuit boards. In this domain the circuit board is monitored by the relevant hardware. The conditions existing in the circuit board could then be written to an external file. The expert system component could use this information to diagnose problems in the circuit board.

(3) An interface to another language — this is where some value is computed by another language and then passed into the expert system. This may be necessary where the tool used to build the expert system does not have the ability to compute this value, e.g. a random number generator. This can be achieved in most expert system shells; however, the language is usually restricted to the one that the shell was implemented in. Also, most dialects of AI languages have interfaces to conventional languages.

Expert systems that can only gather information through user responses typically ask a lot of questions. Users may be reluctant to use systems where there is a long question/answer session. Expert system tools which only allow the user to pass information through user questions rely heavily on the user's ability to be comfortable in using the expert system. This has implications for the user interface; a lot of time and effort has to be expended on the interface component of the expert system. Also, if the user is not happy with how he interacts with the system he will be reluctant to use it. The problem is made worse if the expert system is implemented using a shell, where often the knowledge engineer has little control over the design of the interface (see section 5.5 on the user interface).

The idea of embedding expert systems into applications where some other machinery (other than the user interface) gathers the information is a departure from the format of traditional expert systems. Such systems cannot be implemented in tools which cannot handle sources of information contained in formats external to the expert system. The implementation of expert systems in this manner reduces the amount of effort needed to build the user interface since it only has to display the results to the user in an appropriate form and explain their meaning.

5.4 INFERENCING STRATEGIES

An inferencing strategy determines the control of rule firing; in general terms this can be considered as hypothesis or data-driven. In the former approach, normally known as backward chaining, the system examines conclusions that it would like to make and goes in search of evidence to support them. The other strategy, forward chaining, operates by seeing which rules can be fired as a result of the facts in working memory.

The separation between forward and backward chaining systems is not clear-cut and it is unlikely that only one strategy would be used in a particular system. Backward chaining systems require at least one forward chaining rule, such as the 'Goal Rule' in MYCIN (Buchanan & Shortcliffe

1984). This is necessary to create the first hypothesis and from this the search for preconditions to that hypothesis. Also, forward chaining systems may need rules which establish further data; these are essentially backward chaining. However, it is possible to construct rule sets which can be fired in a forward or backward chaining manner.

Expert system shells usually have both forward and backward chaining control strategies, although one of these will usually predominate. In most shells this tends to be backward chaining, although forward chaining rules are used to fire the first backward chaining rule and possibly to display any conclusions to the user. An expert system tool will be better at implementing one control strategy than the other and the knowledge engineer should be aware of what control strategy is suitable for his application. This will usually be determined by the domain. For example, if there are a large number of conclusions in the problem domain then it may be better to adopt a forward chaining strategy since a backward chaining one would involve testing all the possible solutions.

Often the control strategy in an expert system shell will provide a standard control mechanism whether it be forward or backward chaining. The knowledge engineer should be aware that any extra facilities cannot be embedded into the shell. This may be quite restricting since some applications may require extensions to the standard control mechanism, such as meta-rules. Although some expert system shells do provide this facility, it cannot be added to those that do not.

Using a language to build an expert system would require the knowledge engineer to implement the control strategy. This is not as difficult as may seem at first hand; for example, a backward chaining interpreter that controls the firing of production rules can be written in Prolog in a few lines of code.

However, there are two problems in this area. The first relates to the representation scheme for which the control strategy is implemented. For example, implementing a control strategy for a frame system would be far more complex than a backward chaining strategy for production rules. It may involve developing an abductive control methodology where the expert system generates a set of possible causes to explain the problem. However, as well as implementing the control methodology one would also need to build the inheritance mechanism and control for procedural attachment. The knowledge engineer should be aware that the inferencing strategies for frame systems are far more complex than for production rules.

The second problem relates to extending the basic inferencing strategy. For example, suppose the knowledge engineer wanted to include explanation facilities in the expert system; this can only be achieved by integrating them with the inferencing strategies. The knowledge engineer should be aware that developing a basic interpreter may not be adequate for his needs and that extending this to include other facilities would be a major task. The implementation time for extra facilities would be greater for more complex representation schemes. However, at least the languages give the knowledge engineer the option of adding extra facilities which are not present in expert system shells.

5.5 USER INTERFACE

The interface of any product is crucial to its success; it is the means of communication between the user and the expert system. How the user perceives the expert system will be greatly influenced by the interface; if the user finds the system difficult to use he will be unwilling to spend time in learning how to use the tool (see further, Chapter 7).

When building commercial expert systems a large percentage of the programming effort is taken up in designing and implementing the human interface. The production of expert system shells was an attempt to overcome this burden. They aimed to provide a ready-built user interface for the knowledge engineer. However, earlier interfaces in expert system shells tended to be very limited; some had no windowing facilities and all the outputs from the expert system appeared in scroll mode. Others had windowing facilities and manipulation of colour, but the knowledge engineer had little control over these facilities. For example, in some shells a question is always displayed in a window of the same size and colour.

There is a problem of lay-out when displaying any form of information to the user; this is made worse by the size of the normal personal computer (usually used to deliver most expert systems) screen. Earlier tools tried to overcome this by paging; i.e. when one screen length of text has been displayed the user is prompted to page to the next screen of text. However, when paging to the next screen the information contained in the previous screen is lost. Some shells overcame this by writing all the outputs from the expert system into a file which the user could later browse through. This requires the user to exit from the expert system before viewing the file; however, this may not enable the user to complete the remainder of the consultation unless he can save the consultation and continue from the place where he left the session.

The above problem can be solved by the use of a scrollable window which allows the user to page backwards to text already displayed by the expert system. The problem has already been tackled for the personal computer (PC), and windowed environments have been developed which rest on top of the operating system of the PC. The windowed environments provide facilities for creating WIMP (windows, icons, menus and pointers) interfaces. Although these facilities are not provided in an expert system shell, some expert systems are now being implemented to run under well-established windowing environments. This allows the knowledge engineer all the windowing facilities of the environment, e.g. menus, icons, windows, scrollbars, etc.

Using a programming language to develop an expert system will only give the user very limited interface facilities. The knowledge engineer will have to build the expert system using a graphics package which can be integrated with the programming language. Even with a good graphics package a large amount of time will be taken in implementing the interface. In AI languages such as Prolog this would add further complications since they do not usually have direct access to graphics packages. The graphics functions are usually written in the C language and this may mean interfacing the AI language to C and then the graphics package. Even so these graphics packages are not specifically tailored to expert system development in that they do not provide ready-built question windows or conclusion windows. These would have to be programmed using the graphics package. Although this is needed, at present there are not any specific commercial interface tools for expert system development, except the limited user interface facilities provided by expert system shells.

The knowledge engineer needs to know what type of interface he is building given his practical limitations, e.g. the delivery machine; a more elaborate interface can be developed on a workstation rather than on a personal computer. The knowledge engineer may want a graphics interface with icon, windows, menus, etc. However, the expert system may work just as well with an interface where all the text appears in scroll mode; here there is no need to build the interface using the graphics package. The interface of an expert system shell may be quite adequate, though a computer language may provide for more flexibility, albeit with a greater production time.

5.6 THE GENERAL ENVIRONMENT

A general development environment provides facilities that allow the knowledge engineer to quickly develop the expert system. Such an environment would typically include the following facilities:

- compiling
- editing
- listing
- creating
- debugging
- executing the expert system

When the knowledge engineer interacts with the development environment there is no longer a need for him to interact with the operating system of the hardware. All the facilities the knowledge engineer requires are available in the development environment. This is an extension from the traditional programming development methodology which usually involves an edit, compile and run cycle. Earlier expert system shells tended to use this methodology. Any syntax errors could only be detected as the knowledge base was being compiled; if there is an error the user must go through the cycle again. In this environment the knowledge engineer must be familiar with the syntax of the tool before attempting to build the expert system. With complicated expert system tools this may take some time.

Where the expert system tool has an environment the knowledge engineer is shielded from the syntax of the tool. He need not worry about defining the syntax of the tool; any such errors are detected by the system as soon as they are typed in by the user. The environment might also fill in any keywords used in the knowledge base. In AI computer languages there also seems to be a trend towards providing environments; however they do not have any facilities that allow the knowledge engineer to build the expert systems (such as forms for defining questions or a structured manner to view the knowledge base), but merely include facilities such as loading, saving, compiling and editing knowledge bases.

Although the general environment the tool provides should be considered in selecting a tool to build an expert system, the importance of it will be determined by the type of computer the knowledge engineer is using. For example, if the knowledge engineer is using a workstation where he has the use of a multiple-windowed environment already built into the machinery then the lack of environment in the expert system tool is not such a crucial factor, since he can edit the knowledge base in one window and compile it in another. However, on a personal computer the issue becomes more important since most of them do not have an in-built windowed environment. This means that the knowledge engineer must always exit from the editor before he can compile the knowledge base, etc. This process can cause considerable time delays in building the expert system.

Although most of the facilities provided in the build environment are useful and aid rapid development of expert systems, a note of caution should be passed on how the knowledge base is created using expert system shells. At first when the knowledge engineer is not familiar with the tool the build facility of the environment allows the knowledge engineer to quickly learn how to use the tool. However, once the knowledge engineer becomes more familiar with the tool this facility may often hinder him. This is mainly because the build environment only allows the user to develop the knowledge base in a structured manner; often it is quicker to build the knowledge base using a screen editor since it provides far greater flexibility. Thus if the expert system does not also have an option to create the knowledge base using a screen editor, this can be quite restricting.

5.7 DEBUGGING FACILITIES

Debugging facilities provide the knowledge engineer with tools to quickly test and verify the correctness of the knowledge base. Without some form of debugging facilities the knowledge engineer will find it difficult to determine what rules are being fired and how they impact on the conclusions inferred by the expert system. The three essential features of debugging one should look for in an expert system tool are:

(1)   A trace facility — this shows the control flow of the expert system; it would show any rules that are being fired or any conclusions placed

into working memory. This is often a sequential trace of all the
statements that are being executed in the knowledge base.

(2)   Instantiation of variables — as well as needing to know what state-
      ments are being executed one also needs to know the values of the
      variables in the statements.

(3)   Break facility — the trace facility limits the knowledge engineer to
      viewing only what is being executed by the expert system. However,
      at times, the knowledge engineer may also want to view other variables
      which are not in the current control flow of the expert system. Break
      points allow the knowledge engineer to do this by halting the execution
      of the expert system and then examining the values of other variables
      in the knowledge base.

Some expert system shells have no debugging facilities and in most others
they are inadequate. Very few shells have a formal tracing facility which
provides information on the control flow of the expert system and the values
of variables during the execution of the knowledge base. Although some
shells do have break facilities, the presentation of these is inadequate, i.e.
one can only view one variable at a time and there is no command to list
the values of all the variables in the knowledge base. Often the presentation
of the variables requires that the knowledge engineer use a pen and paper
to record the values of previous variables presented. In other shells one can
only view the values of the variables after the execution of the knowledge
base, not while it is being executed.

Conventional programming languages such as Pascal or C have only
limited debugging facilities, none of which is specifically tailored to expert
system development. The programmer would normally have to rely on write
statements in his program code to determine any errors. However, AI
languages do have formal trace and break facilities which are adequate
to debug programs, but the facilities are not centred on expert system
development, i.e. they would not show what rules are being fired but show
the function that is being called.

Expert system tools require a windowed debugging environment which
has facilities tailored to expert system development. The environment may
have a formal trace in one window, the rules that are being fired in another,
an interface window for questions posed to the user and for setting break-
points, and a window to view what is being asserted into working memory.
Although all these facilities will not be found in a single expert system tool,
in selecting a tool one should be satisfied that the debugging facilities are
adequate for one's needs.

As mentioned earlier, most expert system shells do not have adequate
debugging facilities, but, although they are essential to quickly build the
expert system, this should not preclude the knowledge engineer from
selecting one of these shells to build an expert system. Other facilities of
the tool such as knowledge representation scheme, inferencing, etc. may
outweigh this disability. In the worst case, write statements can also be
used in expert system shells to debug, as is the norm for conventional

programming languages. However, the knowledge engineer should be aware that this is rather more difficult in expert system programs since the control flow, unlike in conventional languages, is not entirely sequential. For example, a rule at the head of the knowledge base may fire a rule which is located towards the end of the knowledge base.

5.8 EXTERNAL INTERFACES

External interfaces to expert system tools allow the user to exchange information between the expert system and different applications/languages and provide mechanisms to integrate the code generated from the external interface to the expert system tool. External interfaces can be used to develop operations that cannot be implemented in an expert system tool, or where it is too difficult or inefficient to implement in the expert system tool, e.g. a random number generator. An external interface can provide the means to overcome this difficulty by writing the relevant code using the language and then passing this information into the expert system tool via the external interface.

There are a variety of external interfaces, the most common of which is a computer language interface to an expert system tool. For example, both AI languages and expert system shells have external interfaces to languages such as C, Pascal and Cobol. An external interface may also exist between different expert system tools, e.g. Prolog can be interfaced to various expert system shells or between database packages. For the implications of this see section 5.9 on database facilities.

An external interface may also call other expert systems and applications which execute directly from the host computer's operating system. This would provide a means of different expert system applications communicating with each other. For example, a health advisor expert system could communicate with a nutrition expert system to make some conclusion. An external interface may also be useful for applying some form of graphics facilities into the expert system. The interface would allow the graphics programs created to be called from within the expert system tool.

A large number of expert system shells do have some external interfaces. This is usually to the language that the expert system shell was written in, and in most cases this is adequate to implement the functionality required. However, no changes can be made to the representation scheme and inferencing strategies using the external interface. One of the main problems the knowledge engineer should consider is how variables are passed from the application to the expert system tool using the interface. The most common way of achieving this is through specially formatted files. The file will normally include a series of assignment statements for a particular variable in the expert system shell. This is then read into the expert system shell by a particular command. Other implementations of external functions may involve having a definition of the external procedure in the expert system tool (although the code is not present in the expert system shell). In order to obtain a value using the external interface one makes a call to that function with the appropriate variables.

The first method using files provides more flexibility because it allows the knowledge engineer to create his own data files and hence pass information into the expert system shell. Also, it allows an expert system to use existing databases as sources of information. The information in the database can be converted into the file format used by the expert system shell and read as data to make conclusions (see section 5.9 on database facilities).

All languages can read data files and there is no need to have a special format for the data file as is required with expert system shells. The facilities provided by external interfaces are not as important for AI languages as they are for expert system tools since languages are more flexible and most of what one wants can be achieved using one language. However, there are cases where external interfaces in a language are essential to the success of the expert system. This problem mainly arises when using an AI language such as Prolog to implement an expert system, i.e. they do not provide any graphics or windowing functions. The graphics packages are usually embedded in the C language. Thus it is critical for an AI language to have a C interface in order to use these graphics packages.

The major problem with some external interfaces is that only one variable at a time can be passed to the expert system tool. This means that if one has written an external function in C which records information using a C structure then most often each of the values in the structure has to be assigned a value to pass it into the expert system shell. Often there is no method of passing the whole C structure as a variable into the shell even if the shell incorporates some form of record structure.

5.9 DATABASE FACILITIES

Database facilities provide the expert system tool with the capability of gathering information from another source in addition to prompting the user via a question-and-answer session. One of the many complaints levelled at expert systems is that they tend to ask too many questions; the use of databases to provide answers to these questions would reduce the number of questions asked. The expert system tool should have an external interface which quickly and efficiently passes information from the database to the expert system. This has been discussed adequately in the previous section.

Many organizations have stores of information which could be used as input to expert systems, e.g. a telecommunications organization may have a database which contains information about customer fault reports. The expert system could use this database to allocate the faults to engineers with the appropriate skills. The application of databases to expert systems would reduce the amount of information provided by the user. This, as well as reducing the programming effort required for the user interface, would also speed up the execution of the expert system.

Large corporate databases are developed on mainframe computers and often managed by commercial database management systems (DBMS). Such databases, which are typically very large, are used for a variety of applications and are subject to frequent change. As a result there seems little point in integrating the existing database to the expert system since this would involve representing the database within the expert system. This would not be very practical in expert system shells since most of the knowledge is coded as rules; however, the information contained in the database would be used as variables to derive conclusions from the rule base. Thus most expert system shells would be incapable of representing this data. The data could be held in a file which was suitably formatted so that the expert system shell could manipulate the data. However, there would be a large overhead in converting the database representation of the information to a file, especially for large databases. In any case it is not practical, since databases are often being updated and modified and there is a need to efficiently manage this process; this can be better achieved by a DBMS. The ideal solution would be to have an external interface to the database; however, most expert system shells are lacking in this department.

Similar problems also arise when integrating a database to a computer language. Although this can be achieved, there is still the problem of maintaining the database. Once again the solution is to have a direct interface between the language and the database. Also, the same issues of passing information between the expert system tool and the database package apply as those discussed in relation to external interfaces.

An expert system may also create a database of information when it is executing. In some cases the amount of data collected may be too large to confine in the working memory of the expert system; what is required is to translate the information to a database so it can be accessed later. This saves having to recalculate the information every time the user wants to consult the expert system.

Another important consideration is the size of the database we are dealing with; as the size of the database increases, the more it is necessary to provide an interface between it and the expert system tool. At present tools only provide interfaces to relatively small databases. When we consider large databases on mainframes there are very few tools to interface to these. Databases provide rich sources of information and could be used as input to expert system tools for various applications, e.g. decision support, help desks and medical advice.

The use of large databases as input data for expert systems is an emerging technology which will be exploited in the forthcoming years, but at present there is no methodology for developing these systems. However, building expert systems integrated with databases on mainframes does provide various advantages.

- multi-user capabilities
- access to database
- integrated and embedded applications
- power and performance

● memory size
● centralized control, maintenance and support
● functionality
● security and back-up.

Implementing expert systems on mainframes is not practical for many organizations; however, this does not mean that they cannot exploit databases held on mainframe computers. The expert system could reside on the personal computer and extract the information from the database on the mainframe via the appropriate communication links.

5.10 EXPLANATION FACILITIES

It is important for an expert system to be able to explain why it reached certain conclusions; indeed the degree to which the expert system is accepted by the user will depend significantly on its ability to explain its reasoning. Users are unwilling to rely on any expert, whether it be human or machine, unless it can explain why it has reached a particular conclusion. This is even more so if the expert is a machine, so the explanations provided by the expert system should be at least as convincing as those provided by the human expert. Explanation facilities are particularly important in domains where the expert system is asked to make judgements affecting human life. In this case the diagnosis will not be accepted without detailed explanation, especially if the expert system disagrees with the human expert.

The basic explanation facilities provided by an expert system should include why it came to a particular conclusion and how it is going to achieve a particular goal. In the 'why' explanation the rules which have been used to derive the conclusions should be presented to the user. In the 'how' explanation the rules that will be used to achieve the goal should be presented to the user. In both cases there should be a translation from the syntax of the expert system rules to a form that is more readily understandable by the user, i.e. natural language.

Explanations in current expert systems typically consist of a trace of the rules in the reasoning process. Such traces only provide the users with a logical proof of the correctness of conclusions made by the system. They may not necessarily provide him with the kind of understanding he is actually seeking in order to judge whether or not to accept the system's advice. Unfortunately, little is known about what constitutes an acceptable explanation for users with different tasks.

When experts explain conclusions they tend to concentrate on helping the user understand the solution space and accept the expert's advice rather than providing any detailed account of the expert's reasoning. For example, experts describe the solution and indicate which advice is appropriate, i.e. they do not give causal reasoning — it consists of a typical 'because that is why'. At present this form of explanation is not available in expert system tools and is a current research topic. We shall concentrate on the 'how' and 'why' explanation facilities mentioned above.

In a large number of expert system shells there is a confusion between providing basic explanation facilities and explanations related to user questions. For example, some expert system shells only have facilities to display additional text if the user cannot understand a question. In other shells it may show the status (true or false) of all the conditions at that particular node of the goal tree. However, these facilities do not in fact aid the user to understand why the expert system came to a particular conclusion.

Explanation facilities provided by other expert system shells are quite crude and it is often difficult for the user to make any connection between the information displayed and the conclusions reached. One of the reasons for this is that the rules are not translated to natural language. Explanation facilities can sometimes be used as an aid to debugging the expert system by seeing what rules are being fired. However, this is in no way a substitute for formal debugging facilities (outlined in section 5.7) required to implement the expert system. The explanation provided by most shells is of little use for debugging when developing anything other than simple systems.

Languages used for building expert systems do not have any explanation facilities. However, they do provide the knowledge engineer with the flexibility of incorporating this facility into the system, albeit with some programming effort. In expert system shells, if this facility is not in-built it cannot be programmed into the system.

5.11 CONCLUSIONS

The expert system tool selected to build the expert system should make the stage of implementation as easy as possible. If all the facilities required by the knowledge engineer are contained in an expert system shell then there is no reason why he should not use this to develop the expert system. However, the main problem encountered in using a shell is that one is restricted to one knowledge representation scheme and inferencing technique. The flexibility of the expert system is limited to the facilities provided by the expert system shell. The use of a programming language overcomes this problem; however, with the greater flexibility provided by the language comes the drawback of having to program all the facilities that are required. This can be a time-consuming task, especially when considering the programming effort required for the user interface.

The main beneficial facility provided by the expert system shell is the user interface. The inference engine and knowledge representation formalism can be quite easily programmed using a computing language. This method provides greater flexibility in adding other features which are not often incorporated in an expert system shell, e.g. meta-rules or explanation facilities.

The amount of time available to build the expert system is a very important factor, and often time constraints will prescribe an implementation using an expert system shell. Expert system shells allow for quick development of the system because most of the facilities are already programmed. Expert system shells may be used to build quick prototypes of expert systems; this may reveal many of the problems that will be encountered when completing the final implementation. This may lead to development of the expert system using a programming language. This also applies to knowledge-engineering tools, although a greater effort is needed to learn these tools.

The aim of this chapter has been to investigate the use of expert system tools for building traditional expert systems (i.e. where the knowledge can be transferred to IF ... THEN conditions or represented in a frame structure). However, it should be noted that expert system shells are mainly limited to building this type of system. They are not flexible enough for building other types of knowledge-based system, e.g. natural language systems, vision systems or planning systems. The main problem is that they cannot handle the flexibility of representation schemes and inferencing strategies required for other knowledge-based systems.

References

Brachman, R. J., & Schmolze, J. G. (1985) An overview of the KL-ONE knowledge representation system. *Cognitive Science* **9** (2) 171–216

Buchanan, B. G., & Shortliffe, E. H. (1984) *Rule based expert systems.* Addison-Wesley, Reading, MA

Ishaq, K. P., & Beaumont, A. J. (1988) A meta rule oriented expert system. British Telecom Research Labs, Martlesham Heath, Ipswich R&T Internal Memo

Ramsey, C. L., Reggia, J. A., Nau, D. S., & Ferrentino, A. (1986) A comparative analysis of methods for expert systems. *International Journal of Man–Machine Studies* **24** (5) 475–499

Acknowledgements

I would like to thank the Director of Research at British Telecom Research Labs for permission to publish this paper.

6

An expert system for ship evaluation and design

Edwin P. Curran and Felix A. Schmidt

6.1 BACKGROUND

One of the as yet unanswered questions facing AI researchers is — what is the best way to build an expert system? Is there a strategy that can be used universally or does the application domain area influence the way the system is constructed? Clearly, the expert system should be reliable and possess the property that its knowledge base can be easily maintained. For example, in the case of a system which advises on personal taxation, not only must the advice given be accurate but the knowledge base must be able to be updated without difficulty, to take account of changes in tax allowances, etc. announced annually in the budget. (For an interesting account on the reliability of expert systems see Bundy 1987.)

At the time of writing, well over 1000 expert systems of varying degrees of usefulness have been built (*CRI Directory of Expert Systems* 1989), but as yet no standard methodology has emerged for developing a knowledge base for use in an expert system. A similar problem surfaced with conventional programs in the 1960s, where the production of large software systems needed to be controlled very carefully, since development was usually carried out by several groups of people. This led to the emergence of a new discipline called software engineering.

Various methodologies for conventional software development exist, some of which are very formal. However, two points do emerge as principles for good software engineering:

- *modularity*, i.e. decomposition into simpler entities called modules. A module represents a single identifiable conceptual unit of a system.
- *localization*. The contents of each module are unaware of the contents of the other modules. Communication is through a well-defined interface only.

In recognition of the absence of any clearly defined development methodology for expert systems, the CCTA in 1988 launched a UK national initiative, GEMINI (Government expert systems methodology initiative), to develop a methodology for building expert systems, hopefully in such a way as to allow evolution and integration with the already existing SSADM (structured systems analysis and design methodology) approach, which is now widely accepted in conventional program design. Many expert systems to date have been developed without giving sufficient thought to the future maintenance of the knowledge base, and as its size grows, control of the project becomes increasingly difficult owing to ill-defined stages of development. Those involved in the GEMINI project are of the opinion that 'there is little fundamental difference between conventional systems and knowledge based systems in terms of the system development and maintenance lifecycle' (Montgomery 1988). It is only fair to point out that this is not an entirely universal viewpoint. For example, Partridge & Wilks (1987) argue that the conventional methodology of software engineering is inappropriate to AI. For a more comprehensive discussion of current methodologies and the comparison between AI and software engineering approaches the reader is advised to consult Partridge & Wilks (1987), Ford (1987) and references therein.

Prototyping has been identified as having a significant role in expert system development. This is a useful way to allow the expert to view the (as yet incomplete) expert system and obtain his/her feedback on the expertise displayed. A disadvantage can be that control of the knowledge base development is not structured but tends to be at the whim of the expert. Prototyping can be categorized into three groups (Ince 1988):

- throw-it-away prototyping
- evolutionary prototyping
- incremental prototyping

The second approach is diametrically opposed to currently accepted conventional software development techniques. Its proponents argue that this is the best way to cope with changing user requirements. An ongoing development of the system and its specification occurs while the system is being built in consultation with the expert. With incremental prototyping the system is built one part at a time but is based on one overall design. The software design changes on a continuous basis in evolutionary prototyping. In both these approaches the system increases in size as development takes place but the control and management of incremental prototypes are easier. Throw-it-away prototypes are constructed mainly to allow a critical evaluation of the proposed system. With their life being of rather limited duration, considerations such as maintainability and documentation assume less significant roles. The actual system can then be implemented sometimes using a completely different environment, once the requirements have been established via the prototype. Clearly this type of prototype must be able to be constructed quickly if the approach is to have any merit.

A recent study funded by the SERC (Cullen & Bryman 1988) has shown that almost 18 per cent of the sample, consisting of around seventy operational expert systems in the UK and America, admitted to using an ad hoc approach to development. About 38% used fast prototyping, where the knowledge was obtained from the expert(s) and the partially built system used as an aid to further knowledge refinement. A further 24.5% adopted an evolutionary approach with an iterative development process over a prolonged period. It is interesting to note that Cullen and Bryman (1988) remark that '. . . however many of the fast prototyping systems involved very little knowledge engineering . . .'

It is against this background — which has, for the sake of brevity, only outlined the issues mentioned rather than treating them in depth — that we want to describe our current work. The expert system that is under construction is aimed at users in the marine transport world, with the intention of providing a tool to aid the process of ship evaluation and design. An essential part of any such system is the provision of graphical output/input and this is described later in the chapter.

Our approach to designing the knowledge base(s) has been to develop a hierarchy of factors, which we give in more detail in section 6.4. Hierarchical approaches have been applied to naval and merchant ship design and/or their operation both in the USA and in Europe with favourable results (Leopold & Reuter 1971, Schmidt 1983, 1985, 1988, Russon & Streifer 1985, Smith *et al.* 1987). These methods have a distinct bias towards planning for operation, with multi-attribute criteria being used for design evaluation. Later we will describe our value system for ship evaluation.

This approach has resulted in a twofold advantage. Firstly, we have been able to adopt 'incremental prototyping' (Ince 1988), thus allowing better development control. Secondly, it has been easier to determine how to divide the knowledge into separate knowledge bases, thus adhering to the software engineering principles of modularity and localization mentioned earlier.

6.2 REVIEW OF EXPERT SYSTEMS IN MARINE TRANSPORT

Marine applications can be divided into two groups — systems for on-board use and those for shore-based design work. In the quest for evermore efficient, cost-effective ships, AI techniques are being applied with success to many tasks previously carried out by humans, thus allowing ships to go to sea with fewer crew. The members of the reduced size crew can be assigned to less mundane, less repetitive jobs. The system MEMEX (Cooper *et al.* 1987) can predict the effect on fuel consumption of defects such as a worn pump or a plugged injection nozzle. Another system in existence advises on the best way to store cargo in order to reduce handling costs (Dillingham & Perakis 1987). Other systems are designed to train crew in the operation of steam propulsion plants and in the debugging of electrical circuits. For other examples the reader is referred to Biancardi (1988) and Bremdal & Zeuthen (1988).

One of the earliest attempts to apply an expert system to marine design is described by Bremdal (1985). A system called STABRIG was developed with the aim of being able to act as an intelligent assistant to the designers of semi-submersible rigs. As the author points out, more development of the system is required, but the main justification for the work is that it establishes the viability of an expert systems approach to marine design.

Akagi *et al.* (1988) have developed an expert CAD system to aid in the design of marine power plants. Their design process consisted of:

(1) defining the purpose of the system
(2) searching for possible design solutions
(3) determining an acceptable design
(4) optimizing the design.

It is in this type of application that we see AI techniques interfacing with conventional programming. The design knowledge is formulated into rules and written in Lisp. Marine engineering data are represented using frames. For a main engine the frame would consist of a number of slots, each containing an item of information such as type of engine, cylinder size, etc. The optimization of the design is described in the paper (Akagi *et al.* 1988) and is implemented in Fortran code which can be called as required.

Traditional ship design (Evans 1959) can be thought of as a spiral beginning with conceptual design (including such things as mission requirements, ship proportions, method of powering and cost estimates), followed by preliminary design, contract design and finally detailed design with working drawings. See also Andrews (1981) for a view of this traditional design which includes the concept of time. The procedure, although extensively used, has been criticized by Erichsen (1982).

Zangemeister (1970) and Keusch (1972) apply morphological analysis in conjunction with systems design whilst Leopold & Reuter (1971), Schmidt (1983, 1985, 1988) and Calkins (1988) extend the application to systems and ship design. This is viewed as finding a set of essential parts, and knowing the desired behaviour of the proposed ship, to be able to specify a unique relationship between the parts. In his paper, Calkins goes on to examine various models which have been used for design or as an aid to ship design. Calkin's group at the University of Washington aim to integrate many of the currently available technologies such as supercomputers, high-level graphics workstations and expert systems with the eventual goal of automated optimum design. This project is certainly an ambitious one and its outcome is eagerly awaited.

6.3 CURRENT WORK

6.3.1 Statement of aims

Our goal is an integrated system for the design and operational evaluation of marine transport vehicles where the main components are:

● An expert system offering menus of major elements of trades, services, constraints and mission requirements from which the user can select and combine at random into activity sets for the vessel concerned. These sets will have to accurately describe existing ship types and their operation and simultaneously offer the possibility to search for and outline new ones.
● A computer-aided design environment for graphical output/input and to assist with proven algorithmic naval architectural computations.

The search for more 'efficient' ships in conjunction with losses of experienced staff due to the reduction of ship building capacity, fleets and therefore design, operational and seagoing personnel necessitates:

● emphasis on operational efficiency and trading flexibility for the ship, particularly during conceptual design, and
● some means to capture, express and make use of operational and design experience which may otherwise be unobtainable.

Both cases involve the acquisition, storage,-presentation and modelling of knowledge, i.e. knowledge engineering. The move towards using the application of AI in ship building, off-shore engineering and marine operations represents a new and invigorating challenge as well as a necessity.

The resource requirements of ship operation can be summarized as shown in Fig. 6.1. Cost and revenue includes all financial transactions involved in the operation of the vessel. Service ability of the ship considers in detail the services the craft may offer to its owner or charterer, impedances to its operation, as well as its mission requirements, which will influence the ship's general arrangement, equipment, the technology installed to aid operation and the training standard required of the crew. Utility of the cargo section identifies the components of the ship and their attributes which enable it to render the services above. Propulsion and machinery systems, manning and habitability together with unquantifiable factors can be gathered under the heading of support of operation since they are concerned with the 'support systems' that the vessel requires for successful operation.

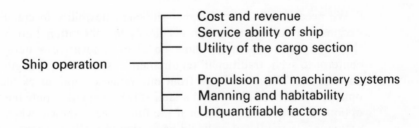

Fig. 6.1 — Resource requirements of ship operation (Schmidt & Curran 1988)

In the remainder of the chapter we will try to show how we obtained the knowledge, how that knowledge was structured and our approach to prototyping. The acquisition of the knowledge has not, so far, been a major obstacle. This may be attributed in large measure to the co-author whose domain knowledge includes marine transport vehicles and ship design. Certainly the literature on the subject has labelled knowledge acquisition as 'the largest bottle-neck in the development of expert systems' (Olson & Rueter 1987), but this has not yet applied in our case. In cases where the knowledge engineer is working with a 'reluctant' domain expert, knowledge elicitation would certainly cause more difficulties. We are convinced that it is essential for at least one domain expert to be committed to the project, as is the case in this work.

6.3.2 Approach and methodology

We are not in a position to propose a definitive methodology as such for the development of expert systems, but in our work we have borne in mind the following:

● Controlled development of the knowledge base — this has been possible since we have been able to work to an overall design.
● Encapsulation of knowledge in distinct knowledge bases (this is our attempt to implement the localization principle mentioned in the background section).
● The need to allow incorporation of good quality interactive graphics, so that a designer can see how his proposed ship is developing.
● The need to allow, particularly for the design of ships, for good human–computer interaction — e.g. use of menus to present options; allowing presentation of secondary menus where the user has selected a 'don't know' option in the first menu.
● Achieving a balance between being over-prescriptive about options occurring on menus and allowing the user too much scope.
● For the design of ships, the possibility needs to be considered of allowing construction to be made from predefined pieces — i.e. primitives, parts and patterns need to be included into the design development. This, at some later stage, will tie in with production requirements.

We need to allow the designer sufficient flexibility to create new ship designs and not constrain him needlessly to conventional approaches. On the other hand, no matter how novel or innovative a design, it must conform to such 'traditional' requirements as stability, strength and cargo friendliness. Where a choice from one range of options excludes certain options which are presented at a later stage, then either only the 'permitted options' should be displayed or if the full range is shown, when an invalid option is selected the user should be invited to reselect. There is a potential problem with the first option — if a new ship is being designed, who is to say what options are 'permitted' for a given parameter? This problem was not completely resolved before we began to build the knowledge base.

6.3.3 Choice of tool/language
In the SERC-funded study (Cullen & Bryman 1988) it was discovered that:

- 47% of the sample used commercially available shells.
- 30% of the sample used languages like C and Pascal.
- 11% of the sample used AI languages, e.g. Lisp.
- 3% of the sample used toolkits like KEE.

A majority of systems, 40%, were developed to be run on a personal computer with 11% designed for use on a dedicated workstation, and 31% able to run on PCs or a mainframe.

While the use of a commercial shell as a tool for building expert systems may be a little restrictive (though perhaps this is less so with modern shells), the advantages are:

- Ability of proposed system to run on 'standard' PCs.
- Increase in speed of development (provided a suitable shell is being used).
- A standard user interface is provided and nowadays the provision of several conventional programming language interfaces is becoming the norm, allowing routines to be written in, for example, C which can then be called up as required during a consultation.
- The builder can concentrate on the knowledge-engineering aspects of the project, with the inferencing strategy being carried out by the shell. Control of this strategy is crucial to a successful implementation of an expert system using a shell.

The option of using toolkits such as ART or KEE was not available to us.

The shell which we eventually decided on was Xi Plus. This is a rule-based shell which is not designed to handle probability. The features which we found most attractive were:

(1) Menu presentation of options.
(2) Multiple-choice menus, where more than one option in a given menu could be chosen.
(3) Backward and forward chaining capability, with control being possible over the inferencing strategy used. Backward chaining is the predominant inferencing technique used. Forward chaining (i.e. data-driven reasoning) can be switched on for selected rules or for an entire consultation. The shell uses an agenda (list of tasks stored in the order to be executed) to find out the next task to perform. It is possible for the knowledge engineer to place tasks on the agenda in more complex applications.
(4) Interfaces provided allow routines to be written in a conventional programming language (useful for numerical optimization).
(5) Xi Plus does allow the display of pictures previously created using,

for example, the GEM package. This is insufficient for our work. However, Xi Plus does permit the passing of data via a file to CADKEY which can then produce the graphics.

(6)   The 'report' facility can potentially be used to store relevant design information as a new ship is being designed.

(7)   The 'is a' and 'of' relationships can be used to create a hierarchical structure and allow a primitive or part to have attributes such as length, breadth, etc.

(8)   The concept of 'floating variables' can help to reduce the number of rules in the knowledge base. Floating variables together with the 'is a' and 'of' constructs are illustrated in the following rule:

IF   Any_ramp is a ramp
AND   type of Any_ramp is slewing
AND   position of Any_ramp is stern
THEN   location of Any_ramp is acceptable

The floating variable in the above rule is Any_ramp and can be any one of the ramps which have been declared in the case of a vessel with RoRo (Roll-on–Roll-off) or ferry-type access. If we suppose that there are four ramps then the above rule replaces four rules of the form

IF   type of rampn is slewing
AND   position of rampn is stern
THEN   location of rampn is acceptable

in which rampn is replaced by ramp1, ramp2, ramp3 and ramp4 in turn. Of course we must declare that:

ramp1 is a ramp
ramp2 is a ramp
ramp3 is a ramp
ramp4 is a ramp

(9)   The knowledge in Xi Plus can be kept in separate knowledge bases which can be loaded into main memory as and when required.
   Drawbacks of Xi Plus (though not for our application) are:

(1)   Approximate reasoning is not possible.

(2)   The inclusive OR operator is not recognized (at least not in its usual form). There is a restricted form of the operator, however, which for the moment at any rate is proving sufficient for us; e.g.

IF   type of ramp1 is side
AND   position of ramp1 is port or starboard

THEN   location of ramp1 is acceptable

is a legitimate rule for Xi Plus whereas

IF   type of ramp1 is side
AND   position of ramp1 is port
OR   position of ramp1 is starboard
THEN   location of ramp1 is acceptable

is invalid syntax since the OR operator is not recognized.

6.4 THE KNOWLEDGE

Precisely what information is required in order to evaluate a marine vehicle design? Are there key factors whose values are critical? Below we list a number of points which need to be addressed:

- Is it possible to select factors which are independent of each other as a basis of evaluation?
- Supposing a number of factors can be identified as having a significant bearing on the design evaluation process, how would it be possible to evaluate alternative solutions? Do factors need to be ranked in order of importance?
- Are economic criteria such as required freight rate (RFR) or net present value (NPV) more important than technical criteria such as minimum steel weight or minimum power? Can economic criteria do justice to a system as complex as a ship? Would it be a better approach to begin with the customer's request for efficient operation and then determine 'essentials' which ensure operational efficiency and technical feasibility and lead to economically justifiable solutions?

Utility analysis as suggested by Zangemeister (1970) has proved to be a helpful approach in selecting the most advantageous design from alternative existing solutions. The logic of this approach is given in Fig. 6.2. This technique is not specific to ship design. Utility analysis can be applied to a wide variety of applications, including commerce, research and government. Problems occurring in such diverse areas as, for example, NASA's space program, selection of equipment or business location, water services, public administration, design of frictional bearings and transport planning have been successfully tackled by the application of utility analysis techniques.

Before launching into the details (which the reader may prefer to omit) we should emphasize that the hierarchy of factors developed is objectively determined whereas the various utility ratings are obtained subjectively, or by consensus, in the assignment of weights to factors, which may vary depending on the intended services that the ship is to provide.

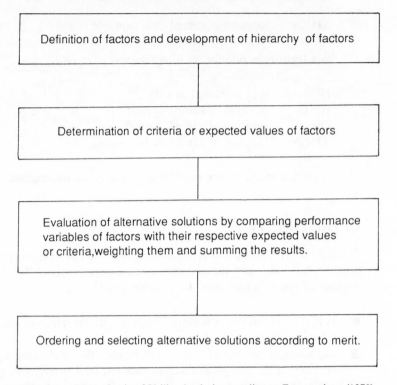

Fig. 6.2 — Macro-Logic of Utility Analysis according to Zangemeister (1970).

6.4.1 A hierarchy of factors

Zangemeister (1970) states that:

Experience shows that both the determination of factors and their correct ordering within the hierarchy presents considerable difficulties.

We are using the word 'factor' as a generic term to include objectives, attributes, items, variables, performance characteristics such as discharging rate, parameters (these are variables which cannot be influenced by the user, such as environmental constraints to dimensions) and criteria (these are the 'expected values' of factors used to assess performance and are obtained from operational requirements and a sample of efficient modern ships — they do not set limits on the values but are intended only to be used as a guide).

We want to discuss the development of this hierarchy and the relationship between factors. Relationships can be based on technology or on classification. Technological associations are generally described by empirical relationships. Classification is based on affinity between factors and describes common features. Both types are used to order factors vertically and horizontally in the hierarchy. As far as technological relationships are concerned, three types can be identified:

(1)   contentious relationships, e.g. no understow in holds and the requirement for 'tween decks to act as shelf space

(2)   complementary relationships, e.g. low speed and low fuel consumption
(3)   indifferent relationships, e.g. type of main engine installed and the
      hatch covers selected.

These relationships are binary ones and may be asymmetric ($xRy \rightarrow$ not
yRx), symmetric ($xRy \rightarrow yRx$) or indifferent ($x=y$). Asymmetric and
symmetric technological relationships and relationships based on classification may be presented as in Fig. 6.3 to show relationships between group
masses.

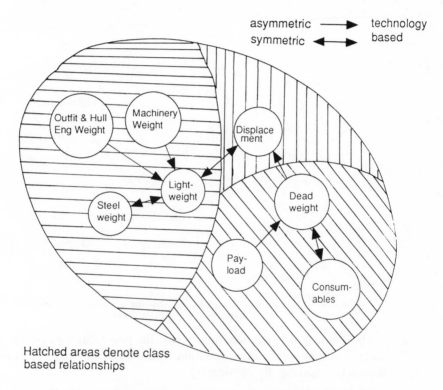

Fig. 6.3 — Asymmetric and symmetric technological Relationships and Relationships based on Classification (Schmidt 1983).

Contentious relationships cause conflict and a compromise solution is
obtained by initially determining the relative importance of the contenders.
(Some factors may need restructuring to ensure the condition of 'almost
independence between factors'.) Factors on the same level of the hierarchy
may not be of equal importance and weights may be assigned accordingly.

Complementary relationships may be symmetric or asymmetric and
generally exist between superior and inferior factors. If a relationship is
symmetric and complementary, $xRy \rightarrow yRx$, only one of the complementary
factors is used in the evaluation, thus reducing the size of the problem
and preventing overweighting of factors. For asymmetric complementary
relationships, ordering can be accomplished by grouping subject-related
subordinate factors in order to determine their common superior factor.

These relationships were used to arrange the factors which represent group masses shown below in Fig. 6.4 in a hierarchy. We will discuss the labelling convention Zij later.

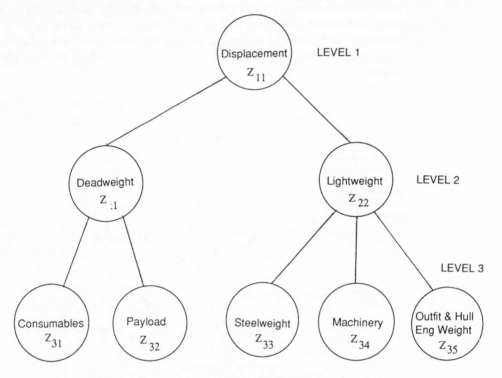

Fig. 6.4 — Hierarchy of Group Masses showing asymmetric complementary Relationships (Schmidt 1983).

This vertical ordering does not exclude the possibility that factors on the same level may still be in competition with each other and so be in need of horizontal ordering. By considering

(1)   the nearest common superior factor
(2)   functional context of factors
(3)   subject-orientated relationships
(4)   common units of measurement

the horizontal ordering can be achieved. The use of these relationships in the development of a hierarchy is summarized in Fig. 6.5.

6.4.2 Scales
To express preferences within sets of factors situated on the same level of the hierarchy, some systematic method of assigning values to factors must be found. (With reference to the example used earlier, steel weight, machinery

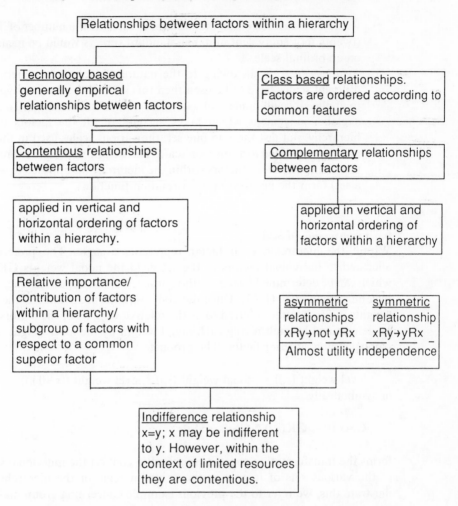

Fig. 6.5 — Relationships between Factors amd their Use in the Development
of a Hierarchy (Schmidt 1983).

weight, outfit and hull-engineering weight form a set of factors, as do
consumables and payload on the third level of the hierarchy and deadweight
and lightweight on the second level.) Various scales can be used:

(1) *Nominal, scale*, e.g. colours or expressions such as 'satisfactory'.
(2) *Ordinal scale*. This allows factors to be ranked by means of numbers.
     The numbers only indicate the direction on the scale, i.e. more, equal
     or less, thus allowing statements such as 'with respect to criterion $K_{.j}$,
     design alternative A_1j has more, equal or less utility than design
     alternative A_2j', i.e. is operationally and commercially more, equally
     or less 'efficient'.
(3) *Interval scale*. This is used when numerical differences between num-
     bers which express preferences are important; e.g. lengths of decks

would be measured on an interval scale, whereas the number of TEUs (twenty foot equivalent units) or standard trailers would be measured on an ordinal scale.

(4)   *Relationship scale.* If, owing to the nature of factors in a hierarchy, different scales have to be used then this scale is the most convenient to apply, since all numerical values are made dimensionless. To make a global judgement which takes account of all the factors in the hierarchy, not just those in one set, the various scales used in the sets must be converted to a common scale. The weighting factors expressing preferences between factors within the hierarchy (as opposed to within a set) form the necessary transformation functions.

6.4.3 Conversion of scales

Within the hierarchy, each factor represents a node. The preferences allocated to individual factors in the set yield the nodal weights $GK(s,j)$, which can be determined by the 'method of successive comparison' suggested by Churchman *et al.* (1957). Once the nodal weights are available, the level weights, $GS(s,j)$, often referred to as the relative weights of the factors, can be determined by multiplying each nodal weight by the level weight of the corresponding superior factor. The product

level weight (s,j) = nodal weight (s,j) * level weight $((s-1),j)$

or symbolically

$$GS(s,j) = GK(s,j) * GS((s-1),j)$$

forms the transformation constant required to convert the individual scales of the various sets of factors to the common scale of the hierarchy. To illustrate this, we refer to the previous example concerning group masses:

(1)   List of factors in the set on the first level
   Number   *Factor*
   11   Displacement
   Preference sequence
   11   Displacement $V_{11} = 1.0$
(2)   List of factors in the set on the second level
   Number   *Factor*
   21   Deadweight
   22   Lightweight
   Preference sequence
   21   Deadweight $V_{21} = 1.0$; $g_{21} = 0.5882$
   22   Lightweight $V_{22} = 0.7$; $g_{22} = 0.4118$

$$\Sigma Vij = 1.7 \quad \Sigma gij = 1.0000$$

This was obtained as follows from a ship-operating viewpoint. Deadweight

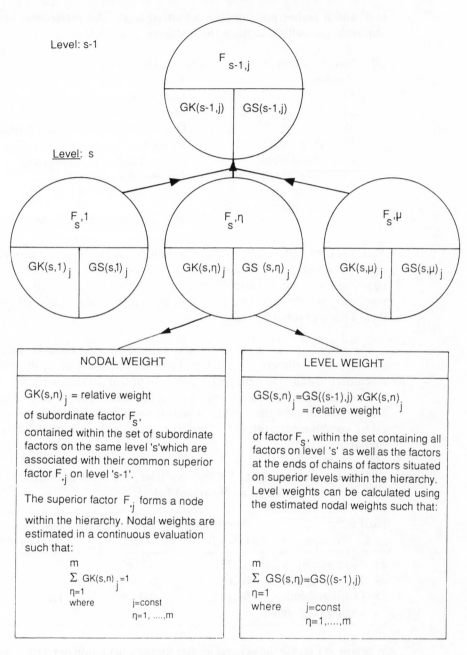

Level: s-1

$$F_{s-1,j}$$

GK(s-1,j)   GS(s-1,j)

Level: s

$$F_s,1$$ $$F_s,\eta$$ $$F_s,\mu$$

GK(s,1)$_j$ GS(s,1)$_j$ GK(s,η)$_j$ GS (s,η)$_j$ GK(s,μ)$_j$ GS(s,μ)$_j$

NODAL WEIGHT	LEVEL WEIGHT

GK(s,n)$_j$ = relative weight of subordinate factor F_s, contained within the set of subordinate factors on the same level 's' which are associated with their common superior factor $F_{.j}$ on level 's-1'.
 	
The superior factor $F_{.j}$ forms a node within the hierarchy. Nodal weights are estimated in a continuous evaluation such that:
 	
$$\sum_{\eta=1}^{m} GK(s,n)_j = 1$$
where   j=const
        n=1, ...,m
	GS(s,n)$_j$=GS((s-1),j) xGK(s,n)$_j$ = relative weight of factor F_s, within the set containing all factors on level 's' as well as the factors at the ends of chains of factors situated on superior levels within the hierarchy. Level weights can be calculated using the estimated nodal weights such that:
	
	$$\sum_{\eta=1}^{m} GS(s,\eta)=GS((s-1),j)$$
	where j=const
	        n=1,....,m

Fig. 6.6 — Logic Format to determine the Relative Weights of Factors (Zange meister 1970).

is more important than lightweight since it determines the amount of cargo carried and therefore the revenue. However, for a given displacement the lightweight determines the deadweight and should therefore be of equal importance. From a shipowner's point of view, deadweight is 'more important' and a higher preference is allocated to it. The preferences are subsequently normalized to form the nodal weights GK(i,j).

(3) List of factors in the second set on the third level

Number	Factor
33	Steel weight
34	Machinery weight
35	Output and hull-engineering weight

Preference		sequence
33	Steel weight	$V_{33} = 1.0\ g_{33} = 0.5263$
34	Machinery weight	$V_{34} = 0.5\ g_{34} = 0.2632$
35	Output and hull-engineering weight	$V_{34} = 0.4\ g_{35} = 0.2105$

$$\Sigma Vij = 1.9;\ \Sigma gij = 1.0000$$

This was obtained as follows. Steel weight forms the largest component of costs on the ships considered. For a given displacement it has also the largest effect on the payload. Therefore it is 'more important' than both the machinery weight and the output and hull-engineering weight taken together. This is ensured by the fact that

$$V_{33} > V_{34} + V_{35}$$

The weight and costs of output and hull-engineering could be similar to that for the machinery installation. From an operating point of view, the machinery installation delivers the power to propel the ship while the output and hull-engineering component plays an important part in cargo handling and port turnaround time. It also affects the suitability of the ship regarding cargo consignments offered. Thus the preferences allocated should be similar:

$$V_{34} > V_{35}$$

With the nodal weights GK(i,j) available, the level or relative weights GS(i,j) can be calculated as illustrated below:

No.	Factor	Nodal weight GK(i,j)	Level weight GS(i,j)	Sum of level weights
33	Steel weight	0.5263	0.2167	
34	Machinery weight	0.2632	0.1084	
35	Outfit and hull-engineering weight	0.2105	0.0867	1.0

We show in Fig. 6.6 the general format for the calculation of relative weights of factors.

6.4.4 Hierarchy development

The previously summarized resource requirements of ship operation, Fig. 6.1, in particular 'Service Ability of Ship' and 'Utility of Cargo Section', were selected, reconsidered and expanded. This resulted in a hierarchy of factors which at a depth of seven levels yielded sufficient detail for conceptual design. Three of these levels are shown in Fig. 6.7.

Additional advantages are that the distinct and sequential 'disciplines' of

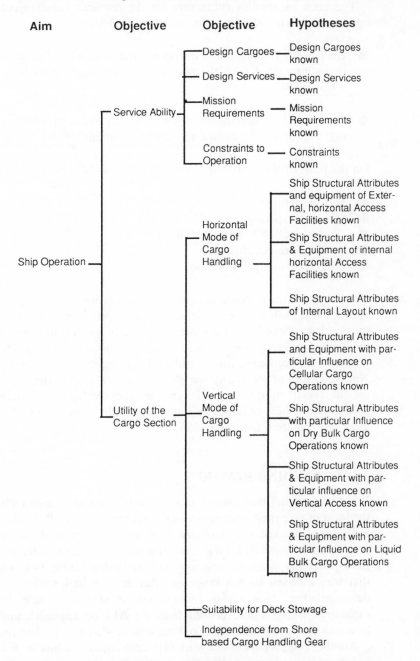

Fig. 6.7 — Part of the Hierarchy of Factors showing three Levels (compare with Figure 6.1).

conceptual, preliminary and detailed design become a continuum, and thus traditional restrictions placed on the designer can be lifted. Hierarchical planning empowers him with a top-down approach which assists in problem definition as a prerequisite to successful solution.

The need to identify subfactors for the resource requirements of ship operation shown in Fig. 6.1 precluded an analysis of:

● the handling, storage and transport characteristics of cargoes and how these interacted with the ship's cargo and payload system (Schmidt 1983, 1988)

● the general arrangements of some 60 ship types of which more than 600 were built and have seen service (Schmidt 1983).

On the basis of these analyses, individual hierarchies were developed for:

● RoRo operation
● container operation
● dry and wet bulk cargo operation
● general cargo operation
● refrigerated cargo operation.

These mapped the interaction between the operation of the marine transport vehicles and their cargoes. The analysis also provided criteria to evaluate the performance of factors at some later stage of the development. Therefore by means of hierarchies a very complex and extensive multi-attribute problem was converted into a multitude of one-dimensional subproblems. Not all factors apply to any one ship. However, true to the implication of the 'universal' morphologic set, the designer/evaluator can select which particular attribute or factor he wants to include in the craft under development or evaluation (Schmidt 1983, 1985).

6.5 CONCLUDING REMARKS

It is not our belief that the utilization of artificial intelligence techniques in the form of an expert system is a universal panacea for all problems. There are already in existence perfectly good optimization programs written in conventional algorithmic languages. It would be foolish to attempt to recode these programs in an AI language such as Prolog simply to be able to say that we had used such a language. Rather, our philosophy has been to determine the areas within the process of marine vehicle design and evaluation which would benefit from an AI-type approach and to then interface them with numerical optimization code as and when required.

Another central part of our work is the provision of a link with a graphics package (in our case CADKEY), which will enable a designer to view the progress of the design. As mentioned in a previous section, a designer must have the freedom to create novel marine vehicle architectures, provided of course that the end product is stable, economically and environmentally feasible, etc. It is therefore imperative that an outline drawing can be produced together with a report containing essential details of the current design.

Our building strategy is not domain-dependent. Earlier work in developing the hierarchy of factors is now paying substantial dividends. It is our belief that the time and effort devoted to finding that it was 'cargo-handling operations' which provided the means to tame the multitude of complementary and conflicting characteristics of ship types and their cargoes has greatly simplified the construction of the knowledge base(s).

The macro-logic of utility analysis is given in Fig. 6.2, and in order to obtain 'expected values' for the purposes of comparison with actual values produced by various factors, a sample of some 60 ships, of which more than 600 have been built, has been used. Clearly the process of unitization and associated cargo-handling techniques of building new ships and breaking old ones is an ongoing one and so the criteria or 'expected values' must be able to be updated. This does not present a problem when using Xi Plus.

We have been able to work to an overall design since the hierarchical structure was determined before we began building the knowledge base. This has proved to be beneficial since it enabled us to control the development/acquisition of the knowledge and indicated that it was feasible to separate the knowledge into separate knowledge bases which could be chained together, thus not exceeding the 640K memory restriction of the PC in use. Development of the rules together with the graphics link is ongoing (Schmidt & Curran 1988). The end result will be a versatile design/evaluation tool which has obvious commercial applications.

REFERENCES

Akagi, S., Tanaka, T., & Kubonishi, H. (1988) An expert CAD system for the design of marine power plants using artificial intelligence. *Japanese Society of Mechanical Engineers International Journal Series III* **31** (1) 149–156

Andrews, D. (1981) Creative ship design. *The Naval Architect* (November)

Biancardi, C. G. (1988) Applications of artificial intelligence in the management of marine operations. *Permanent International Association of Navigation Congress Bulletin* **60** 115–125

Bremdal, B. A. (1985) Marine design theory and the application of expert systems in marine design. In: *Computer applications in the automation of shipyard operation and ship design* vol V. North-Holland/Elsevier, Amsterdam

Bremdal, B. A., & Zeuthen, S. (1988) Intelligent computer aid in marine design and ocean engineering. In: *The Society of Naval Architects and Marine Engineers, Spring Meeting/STAR Symposium/3rd.* IMSDC, Pittsburgh, PA

Bundy, A. (1987) How to improve the reliability of expert systems. In: Moralee, D. S. (ed.) *Research and development in expert systems* vol. IV. Cambridge University Press, Cambridge

Calkins, D. E. (1988) Ship synthesis model morphology. In: *The Society of Naval Architects and Marine Engineers, Spring Meeting/STAR Symposium/ 3rd*. IMSDC, Pittsburgh, PA

Churchman, C. W., Ackoff, R. L., & Arnoff, E. L. (1957) *Introduction to operations research*. Wiley, London

Cooper, R. B., Dickerson, D. J., Selfridge, M., & Williams, K. E. (1987) *MEMEX: an expert system for vessel energy management, user's manual and final report*. Technical report to maritime administration US Department of Transportation No. MA-RD-770-87008

CRI Directory of Expert Systems (1989) Learned Information, Oxford

Cullen, J., & Bryman, A. (1988) The knowledge acquisition bottleneck: time for reassessment? *Expert Systems* **5** (3) 216–225

Dillingham, J. T., & Perakis, A. N. (1987) Expert stowage planning. In: *Proceedings of Fleet Management Technology Conference, Baltimore, MD, 5–6 May*

Erichsen, S. (1982) *Design of transport by sea*. IMSDC, Pittsburgh, PA

Evans, J. H. (1959) Basic design concepts. *American Society of Naval Engineers Journal* **71** (4)

Ford, L. (1987) Artificial intelligence and software engineering: a tutorial introduction to their relationship. *Artificial intelligence Review* **1** (4) 255–273

Ince, D. (1988) *Software development: fashioning the baroque*. Oxford Science, Oxford

Keusch, W. (1972) *Entwicklung einer Gleitlaqerreihe im Baukastenprinzip*. PhD thesis, Technical University, Berlin

Leopold, R., & Reuter, W. (1971) *Three winning designs — FDL, LHA, DD-963: method and selected features*. Society of Naval Architects and Marine Engineers

Montgomery, A. (1988) GEMINI: Government expert systems methodology initiative. In: Kelly, D., & Rector, A. (eds) *Research and development in expert systems*. vol. V. Cambridge University Press, Cambridge

Olson, J. R., & Rueter, H. H. (1987) Extracting expertise from experts: methods for knowledge acquisition. *Expert Systems* **4** (3) 152–168

Partridge, D., & Wilks, Y. (1987) Does AI have a methodology which is different from software engineering? *Artificial Intelligence Review* **1** (2) 111–120

Russon, L., & Streifer, S. (1985) A system engineering approach to support design of the navy's SL-7/T-AKR fast logistics support ship conversions. *Marine Technology* **22** (3) 267–285

Schmidt, F. A. (1983) *Application of utility analysis to the design and operational evaluation of multi-purpose ships*. PhD thesis, CNAA, London

Schmidt, F. A. (1985) The concept of utility analysis and its application to ship design. In: *Ship Design: The Operational Requirement, Nautical Institute & RINA Symposium, London*

Schmidt, F. A. (1988) Cargo and payload systems: full task report 3. In: *UK Efficient Ship Program, Integrated design project, part 3*, Department of Trade and Industry.

Schmidt, F. A., & Curran, E. P. (1988) The application of IKBS systems to ship operation, ship evaluation and ship design. In: *NAV'88–WEMT'88 Symposium: Advances in Ship Operations, Trieste*

Smith, W. F., Kamal, S., & Mistree, F. (1987) The influence of hierarchical decisions on ship design. *Marine Technology* **24** (2) 131–142

Zangemeister, C. (1970) *Nutzwert Analyse in der Systemtechnik*. Wittenmansche, Munich.

7

Human–computer interaction for knowledge-based systems

Terry J. Anderson

7.1 INTRODUCTION

The number of people using interactive knowledge-based systems as tools at work grows daily. The effectiveness of these tools is critically dependent on the quality of the human–computer interface — that part of a computer system which the user sees, hears and communicates with. No matter how complex the knowledge base or how sophisticated the inference engine, it is ultimately the user interface which determines how easily that knowledge can be accessed and employed. While the intricacies of knowledge representation or details of the implementation language may be more intellectually challenging, they are unlikely to have as significant an impact on the user's acceptance of the completed system. A badly designed interface can result in user frustration, increased mistakes in system operation and failure to trust or even to use the system.

Recent years have seen the emergence of human–computer interaction (HCI), a new field that draws on psychology, cognitive science, sociology, linguistics, graphic design and computer science. Its aim is to enhance the usability of software by focusing on people rather than technology, on people's goals and needs, and the kind of tasks they wish to perform (Norman & Draper 1986). The potential contribution of HCI to conventional software systems is now widely recognized (*IEEE Software* 1989) and the case for its explicit incorporation into the traditional software development cycle is cogently argued by Mantei & Teorey (1988). Given that the user interface typically constitutes 30%–50% of both conventional and knowledge-based systems (Baecker & Buxton 1987, Bobrow *et al.* 1986), this is perhaps less than surprising.

It is the aim of this chapter to present the major guidelines of HCI as they apply to the end-user interface of knowledge-based systems (KBS). While major projects commonly employ 'human factors' specialists on their development teams, this royal road to interface development is not economically feasible for the majority of systems, which typically comprise a few hundred rules, anticipate a user base numbered in tens rather than hundreds, and will be created by at most two or three developers. The practical route is to arm the developers with a good awareness of HCI principles, thus enabling them to improve the user acceptability of their own KBS.

The chapter begins with a brief look at the common iterative strategies normally employed in both KBS and interface construction, which pave the way for their parallel development. User psychology is then outlined to give an appreciation of the overall requirements for a good user interface. This is followed by HCI guidelines derived from experiments, from theories of human cognition and from engineering experience on both conventional and knowledge-based systems. Finally the chapter considers the variety of dialogue styles and nature of interface evaluation.

7.2 PROTOYPING

Complete, clear and unambiguous specifications are not normally available for KBSs (Partridge & Wilks 1987). As a result their construction tends to be a highly interactive and dynamic process. Knowledge engineers cannot follow the more predictable conventional software development life-cycle but must rely on prototyping in which initially broad system objectives are iteratively refined. During each iteration, to various degrees, respecification, redesign, re-implementation and re-evaluation take place. The prototyping is not usually 'throw-away', where the prototype code is simply junked after development, nor is it incremental, where the overall structure of the software is reasonably well-known in advance. Rather it is evolutionary, and the system emerges gradually. It is not uncommon for the final prototype to become the production version. It may also be used as specifications where the KBS is to be to re-implemented in more efficient code (Ince 1988).

Similarly, in HCI there is as yet no methodology or set of prescriptions capable of generating specifications for an optimal user interface. HCI development is by nature more analytic than synthetic — something must first be built, then analysed, then iteratively refined (Hartson & Hix 1989). By repeatedly demonstrating and evaluating the user interface, deficiencies can be detected and rectified. As each version of the prototype is completed, it must be reviewed not only by management and those whose expertise it captures, but also by the end-users (Walters & Nielsen 1988) (see section 7.6 on evaluation).

The prototyping medium used by knowledge engineers must support evolutionary development. This is true of most current implementations of Lisp, Prolog or sophisticated expert system shells which allow comparatively easy construction and revision not only of the knowledge base but also of the interface. These tools also tend to be more declarative than procedural, so that the state of a dialogue is explicit and often more readable than in procedural code. Unfortunately, it is still rare for advanced facilities to be provided for HCI. It is to be hoped that tool providers will before long rectify this situation.

Prototyping is a vehicle for refining design; it supplements it but can never become a substitute for it. As yet, HCI can only offer the developer principles and guidelines to help formulate the initial best-guess design and later to identify points for evaluation in each successive version (Draper & Norman 1984). The better the initial design, the fewer the subsequent major alterations and the lower the overall development costs.

7.3 USER PSYCHOLOGY

From the HCI perspective the most crucial component in a computer system is the user. In the past, system developers have used introspection and personal experience to shape the interface, with the result that features they assumed would be simple and obvious often proved obscure and infuriating to the less computer-oriented users. Psychology can produce a more objective picture of how human beings in general process information. This knowledge can attune designers to some fundamental interface requirements and provides a sound starting point for interface design. Research on the perceptual/cognitive system has confirmed the counter-intuitive fact that we humans can absorb only a tiny fraction of the visual, audio and tactile information reaching us from our external environment (Wagner 1988). Where we wish to consider some part of that incoming information, our senses must place it in our short-term memory (STM) which at once enhances and severely restricts our information-processing capacity. STM has a very limited storage capacity, usually rated as 7 ± 2 'chunks', where the size of a 'chunk' is a function of human experience and item complexity. As implied in the use of 'short-term', the period of retention is brief, typically 15 to 30 seconds, though we can extend this by repeating STM contents to ourselves, as when trying to remember a telephone number. STM is not security-conscious; when it is full and receives more information we simply remember the new and forget some of the old. This is undesirable because STM is the only location we have to hold the contingency plans and options which are part of our decision-making process. While our long-term memory (LTM) is an effectively infinite store, we have no conscious control of the path from STM to LTM, a path which is asymmetric, allowing fast read but slow write. This prevents use of LTM for temporary storage.

From these observations follow two central considerations for the interface designer. First, since STM storage is limited and in constant danger of information overload, the interface should minimize its demands on STM, leaving as much spare capacity as possible for decision making. Only information which will help the user make some sort of decision should normally be on the screen. To this end, displays should be kept simple and uncluttered (Otte 1984). Secondly, to maximize what can be stored in STM, meaningful and familiar chunks should be used wherever possible. In practice this entails selecting terms or phrases well-known to the users.

The inherent STM limitations on amount and duration of storage result in a strong psychological desire to end the current task which is constraining the use of STM. This is our desire for 'closure' and explains why users, particularly inexperienced users unfamiliar with a particular system, prefer a sequence of small and simple operations to a single powerful and complex command.

Ideally KBSs should facilitate cooperation of user and machine through a mixed initiative dialogue, a two-way process where 'both parties initiate interaction (ask questions, or set goals) and respond (answer, or carry out investigations)' (Cleal & Heaton 1988, p. 21). For example, the user might wish at any point to have the system retrieve information from a database so that he can decide how the dialogue should best proceed. Not only is such flexibility akin to the way we normally interact with other people, but users much prefer software where they feel in control, able to determine the sequence of events, rather than being obliged to follow rigidly predetermined paths. While novices are willing to be led slowly by a computer system through a highly constrained dialogue, as their system familiarity grows they will want to take the initiative and use the available features in the order they find most convenient.

There are two quite different broad aims for an interface: (1) achieving speed and convenience of use for the practised user and (2) achieving ease of learning and use for the newcomer. Inevitably there will be a trade-off between the two based on how well the designer can 'know the user' (Shneiderman 1987). While user psychology can shed some general light here, for each planned KBS more specific user profiles need to be drawn up. It may often not be possible to produce clear profiles of potential users, but it is important to try. The assessment will normally be made on subjective grounds, on informed guesses and by seeking the opinions of other developers, but it underpins the main assumptions which will determine the nature of the interface.

The three major considerations identified by Sutcliffe (1988) are (1) frequency of use, (2) user experience and (3) typing skills. Where most users will operate the system frequently, speed and convenience should be given a higher priority because here users will develop skills relatively fast. Infrequent or intermittent users (probably the more common KBS usage pattern) will require a more supportive interface, offering clear prompts, guidance about possible next steps and plenty of explanatory text. The greater the users' general level of experience with other computer software, the less crucial become ease of learning and use. Typing skills may seem a mundane consideration, but typing ability, which ranges from 'hunt-and-peck' to touch-typing, greatly influences the anticipated quantity of information input.

The rest of this chapter seeks to set out widely accepted guidelines for HCI design. Confronted by a particular task, the designer may find the guidelines pointing in conflicting directions. Personal judgement and advice from potential users must then be the final arbitrators.

7.4 GUIDELINES FOR HUMAN–COMPUTER INTERACTION

7.4.1 Consistency

Whatever the style of interface adopted, a high level of consistency is desirable. Predictability in the patterns of control and information presentation makes for ease of use and learning (Gardiner and Christie 1987). A limited number of screen lay-outs with consistently placed titles, status information and system messages minimizes any surprises which might intrude on the user's decision making. The standardized use of terminology in prompts, menus and help screens reduces the amount of learning required. Colour can convey useful status information provided it is used consistently, e.g. red for errors or white for user-entered text. The combination of these features in a direct manipulation (or WIMP) interface is undoubtedly one reason for the popularity of this style. Where the KBS development software supports it, it is well worth considering WIMP presentation.

7.4.2 Flexibility

A flexible interface can be varied according to the user's level of skill. A simple but effective technique is to allow the operator to establish explicitly the required level of verbosity; a novice may choose long prompts, the average user may select standard prompts, while an experienced user may prefer terse ones. It should be possible for the user to change the level of prompting at any time to compensate for uneven familiarity with different parts of a system. A less cumbersome variant on this method enables the user implicitly to select either menu or command mode; hitting an arrow key moves a selection bar on a menu, pressing a text key will immediately start command entry. With experience the user will tend to take advantage of the more powerful commands, whether typed in full or abbreviated, but the menu safety net remains reassuringly available to cope with unfamiliar or half-forgotten features.

Flexible interfaces, as outlined above, rarely offer the user more than two or three discrete modes. This contrasts with human–human interaction where we continuously adapt what we say and how we say it to our perception of the listener's level of knowledge and ability. Against such a comparison, flexible interfaces seem very inflexible.

Adaptive interfaces which aim to match their presentation more closely to the continuum of user skills are under development. The user is no longer pigeon-holed as novice, skilled or expert, and provided with a corresponding standard interface mode, as in the flexible interface. Rather, an attempt is made to parallel human interaction by building a user model on the basis of the user's inferred expertise (Carroll & McKendree 1987) (see also Chapter 8). The system can then tailor the interface to suit it to the skills of the particular individual at a specific time. The many unresolved issues of this approach include how to maintain a record of the user's work patterns and help calls, how to evaluate his errors and how to categorize command usage patterns. The task of deducing the user's skills and needs from such a potentially enormous volume of data, representing the information in a comparatively parsimonious knowledge structure, and massaging the interface for optimum efficiency represents a major ongoing research task for cognitive scientists. Take, for example, the specific case of error detection. Before a user action can be classified as an error, a reliable way of recognizing the user's intentions must be identified. This is extremely difficult since all that the KBS sees of the user is key presses or mouse movements, not his puzzled expression as he thumbs through a printed manual.

Compounding the technical difficulties of adaptive interfaces are three major unresolved HCI issues. The first is the desirability of allowing the system to dynamically modify the interface during an interactive session. If the on-screen appearance changes then consistency is reduced. Secondly, users may loose the feeling that they are in control of a system if it is allowed to alter the interface without first asking their permission. Thirdly, while there are many gradations of proficiency among users, it is difficult to see how, in practical terms, more than a limited number of interface modes or levels of explanation can be provided. (The problems of providing explanation facilities are addressed in subsection 7.4.5.)

7.4.3 Continuous feedback and response time

'For every operator action there should be some system feedback' (Shneiderman 1987, p. 61). At all times the user should be aware of (1) where he is in the system, (2) what he has just done and (3) whether or not it was successful. Finally, (4) if a command cannot complete quickly, there should be some indication that work is in progress. Designers of KBSs have in leading wordprocessing and spreadsheet packages some excellent examples of continuous feedback to follow. Typically the name of the file being processed is continuously displayed, the command given or menu option selected is clearly echoed to the screen, success or failure is either visually obvious or an error message appears, and when a slow task is in progress a message such as 'wait' or 'saving' is displayed.

It is important that the speed of feedback should not interrupt the user's flow of thought. Slow response times represent a very common source of user dissatisfaction with KBSs, due in large measure to the inherently slow interpretative techniques widely used in inference engines. While the minimum acceptable delay varies with the task — simple tasks are expected to execute faster than more complex ones — the effective upper limit is set by STM volatility at around 15 seconds. Where fairly complex decisions must be taken by the user, excessively rapid response times can depress overall productivity (successful interactions minus errors) by increasing error rates. Users, it would seem, feel pressurized to respond too quickly and take less care in planning their dialogue (Barber & Lucas 1983).

In KBSs a facility enabling the user to volunteer information offers a double benefit. Not only can it substantially reduce the number of questions which the system will need to ask, and therefore reduce run time, but it can also allow the user to offload information and reduce the risk of STM overload. Since relevant facts may occur unpredictably to the user during an interaction session and claim STM storage, the system should permit volunteering at any time.

7.4.4 Immediate error handling

The user should have the opportunity to interrupt processing and correct a mistake immediately he detects it. STM must otherwise store the error and a plan for its correction. A simple but often committed design mistake is to collect information from the user through a screen form, but constraining field entry to a prescribed order and allowing corrections only after all fields have been entered.

An undo command returns the dialogue to its previous state, and although not always easy or in every case possible to implement (it may not be possible to undelete a knowledge base) is particularly valuable for novices, since it decreases their anxiety level and encourages exploration of the options. Where the user has become lost in the dialogue or, for whatever reason, wants to exit some part of the system, an escape mechanism should exist. It is very comforting to know, for example, that pressing the escape key once will take the dialogue to a previous level and that repetition of the command will eventually lead back to the start point.

Error detection by a KBS is generally of the simple syntactic or 'out of range' type; detection of semantic errors requires user modelling. Error messages need to be as specific and brief as possible, phrased in a simple factual style to indicate the cause of the error and, where possible, offering guidance on how it may be corrected. With a modest additional effort, for example, the message 'File not found' could be replaced with the more context-specific and helpful 'Knowledgebase b:plans5.kb not found. Check plans5.kb is on disc in drive b'.

7.4.5 Explanation and help

KBSs can rarely be deemed to be complete, i.e. to know everything possible about a particular domain. Neither can the knowledge they contain always be categorized simply as right or wrong if conclusions of rules have probability weightings attached. Moreover, no current system comes close to containing the myriad of apparently simple facts which we call common sense. The trustworthiness of a KBS's conclusions therefore is never fully assured. It falls to the user to judge its conclusions and determine if it is sensible to accept them. The purpose of an explanation facility, then, is to enable the KBS to provide sufficient information for the user to understand its reasoning and to discover shortcomings in the knowledge base (Davis and Lenat 1982). Good explanation systems, however, are difficult to achieve.

An explanation needs to be accurate, relevant and presented in a way and at a level of detail which is readily comprehensible to the user. There are many categories of explanation, but the main ones involve explaining *what*, as when defining and clarifying terms; explaining *how*, where a process or structure is described; and explaining *why*, citing reasons or causes to justify either a conclusion or a request for information (Sell 1985). Until the user modelling previously referred to matures and makes possible explanation generation matched to individual needs, KBS developers have in hand a number of rather unsophisticated techniques. The three principle ones are as follows.

First, a piece of explanatory text can be prepared for some or all of the steps in an inference chain, and relevant 'canned' scripts are displayed when explanation is requested. Depending on the quality of the text, this can be a highly effective way of answering 'what' questions and of defining terms. Its primary advantage is simplicity of implementation and flexibility in terms of the detail and nature of explanation provided. The major drawbacks are that (1) the explanation text is the same for all users, (2) it cannot give complete coverage since it is virtually impossible to anticipate every question that may be asked and (3) it requires great care during knowledge base maintenance to ensure that the explanations reflect all revisions.

Secondly, there are form sentences, a type of canned text augmented with actual values, so that the explanation is more relevant to the current task. They are generated by defining output formats in which text strings, which read like parts of a sentence, are interspersed with either textual or numeric variables. Clarke (1989) gives us the following example of how the explanation

> The car requires a visit to the garage since a
> terminal discharge level of 0.0 V indicates a
> faulty battery

could be generated from the form sentence:

> The < singular form of object > requires
> < problem solution > since a < variable > level of
> < value > < variable units > indicates < problem >.

Although the number of form sentences might become substantial in a large system, particularly if the quality of the English grammar is to be maintained, the context sensitivity is highly desirable.

Thirdly, there is execution tracing or 'rule dumping' which provides the most common form of explanation facility. Operationally simple — a record is kept of the answers given by the user and of the rules fired to reach a conclusion — this technique has the important advantage that explanations automatically take account of any changes in the knowledge base. The most obvious shortcoming is that the explanation generated remains no more than a detailed report of the steps followed by the KBS without reference to the underlying problem-solving strategy. Inclusion of canned text to clarify why a particular rule was appropriate at a certain time can go some way towards overcoming this limitation. Attempts to make the trace more readable by presenting the rules in a form closer to natural language than their representation within the knowledge base are no compensation for this inherent weakness.

A human expert, when asked for an explanation, typically moves from the general to the particular, outlining the current goals and problem-solving strategy and pointing out only the most relevant details. This helps the user gain an understanding of the overall problem-solving process. By contrast, the forms of explanation outlined in the foregoing paragraphs normally provide detailed information without an overview. Knowledge about the problem-solving strategies can however be explicitly included in a KBS through meta-rules — rules about rules. In response to a 'why' question, the reasoning in the last fired meta-rule can be reported (Cleal & Heaton 1988). For example, a tutor selecting students for a university course might wish to know why the system is asking for details on a candidate's use of English. The explanation might be as follows:

> Meta-rule 23 requires a candidate's proficiency
> in use of English to be established for
> students educated in a non-English speaking
> country in order to identify language training needs

Such explanations allow the user the enjoyment of probing and understanding the KBS, extending in the process his own knowledge of the problem domain.

The explanation facility of a KBS should provide most of the assistance a user will require. There is, however, still an important place for on-line help, as found in conventional systems. Its function will normally be restricted to presenting canned details of a command or query syntax and should provide both general help, describing the major functions of the system, and help about individual commands or functions. It should be accessible at any point during user interaction and must be accurate and comprehensive. Houghton (1984) provides sound guidelines on developing help text.

Care in the dynamic presentation of help is particularly important. Help is normally requested in order to find and apply a solution to some on-screen problem. Displaying this assistance should cause minimal disruption to the dialogue, otherwise the user may forget some of the details involved. Where screen generation is rapid, pop-up techniques are particularly suitable since they can display help in a dialogue box and then quickly restore the original screen contents.

Printed documentation represents another major source of help, forming an integral component of a KBS. In the HCI literature it is a much observed fact that people consult large software manuals only rarely. The dictum 'when all else fails, read the instructions' seems to apply. In recent years this has led to the widespread practice of providing two manuals with a system. The first is usually in small format and rarely more than 30 pages long. It contains a brief overview of the system followed by an introductory tutorial involving one or more short but realistic 'hands-on' exercises that get the user started. Behavioural studies have shown that such manuals are followed and give users confidence to start using the system. After this they usually try and 'wing it', which should be possible if the interface is well-designed. The second manual, a well-indexed command reference, is still necessary since users will occasionally refer to it when they wish to access more advanced facilities. A worthwhile third item is a quick review listing the commands and their syntax. It is often produced in the form of a folded card which can easily be kept to hand while the system is in use.

7.5 DIALOGUE STYLES

The decision to use menus, command syntax, forms or whatever combination of dialogue styles necessarily comes early in the KBS development process since interface requirements must be considered in the choice of implementation language and hardware. The designer must aim for the best match between the KBS's planned capabilities and the users' needs. If, for example, the system manipulates information which users can most readily assimilate as maps or diagrams, a graphics display is essential.

To date KBS interfaces have been dominated by menus. Although they provide quite tightly constrained system-oriented dialogues, and limit the range of possible responses, they suit novice or intermittent users who need only recognize the options offered. When offered on comparatively powerful microcomputers or workstations, often as part of a direct manipulation interface, the old criticism that menus tend to be slow to use is no longer valid.

Command-oriented interfaces are well-suited to situations where the system will be in frequent use. It becomes reasonable to ask the user to learn the command language to allow rapid use of the system. In practice, however, many people will use their KBSs comparatively infrequently.

A natural language interface might seem an ideal choice for communicating with KBSs. It should afford the user highly expressive power in the language he already knows, and allow him to change the direction of the interaction at will rather than following a prespecified pattern of questions and answers (Sparck-Jones 1985). While the future of KBS interfaces probably does lie with natural language, the level of 'naturalness' provided even in state-of-the-art systems is severely restricted.

There are many reasons why current natural language interfaces cannot be strongly recommended. First, natural language is highly ambiguous, the meaning of a word or phrase being often context-dependent (Hill 1983); 'the battery is flat', 'the sea is flat' and 'they live in a flat'. Secondly, even if the response time from the computationally demanding natural language interface were minimal, the user's input would tend to be wordy, slowing down the interaction rate particularly for those lacking good keyboard skills.

Thirdly, numerical equations are much more succinct and natural for communicating numerical information. Fourthly, natural language responses from a computer could mislead users into unrealistic expectations of systems which in reality will recognize only a limited vocabulary and converse about a narrow domain. 'They rarely accept synonyms and pronouns, never metaphors, and only acknowledge users willing to wear a rigid grammatical straitjacket' (Lenat and Feigenbaum 1989).

7.6 INTERFACE EVALUATION

HCI guidelines provide conceptual tools for interface design and establish general standards for assessing interface quality. As mentioned in section 7.2 on prototyping, evaluation of usability and system functionality should be carried out in parallel on the successive prototype versions. The earlier interface evaluations are arguably the most crucial since they may result in a radical reassessment of the dialogue style. Evaluations towards the end of the development process serve mainly to refine detailed points.

Both objective and subjective measures are involved in interface evaluation. The objective measures include speed of use, frequency of command use and error rates. A range of techniques are available for collecting this information, but two of the least intrusive are video recording and dribble-file analysis. In video recording, tapes of users in action are scrutinized and obvious sticking-points in the system are noted. A dribble-file is a record of the input–output traffic between user and computer and must be manually examined to reveal usage problems. Both these methods tend to be laborious, but they have proved their effectiveness in identifying weak parts of an interface, such as frequently misunderstood message wording or poor error correction facilities.

Subjective measures can provide valuable insight into attitudes and opinions about an interface and also reveal levels of user satisfaction. Chin *et al.* (1988), for instance, have developed a thorough and reliable questionnaire on which the user evaluates aspects such as ease of correcting mistakes or consistency of message positioning on a 1 to 5 scale. Such questionnaires are simple for the user to understand, quick to complete and easy for the designer to analyse. If only rating scales are used, however, they tightly constrain what the user can communicate. It is important, therefore, to give an opportunity for the user to comment freely, either in an open section on the questionnaire or in an informal interview.

7.7 CONCLUSION

HCI is a relatively new field which emphasizes the need to design the interface around the user. Incorporation of the HCI perspective into KBS development is aided by their common use of an iterative development methodology. While KBS developers cannot be expected to become HCI experts, the usability of their final systems can be much enhanced by a good awareness of such guidelines as presented in this chapter. Arguably HCI is too replete with general observations and advice, and somewhat short on theory, precision and methodology. The large volume of ongoing research should ensure that this picture changes rapidly, just as in the last twenty years conventional programming has progressed from a craft using rule-of-thumb guidelines to the discipline of software engineering. Such developments will be particularly welcome as the complexity of KBSs increases and the user base continues to expand.

REFERENCES

Baecker, R. M., & Buxton, W. A. S. (eds) (1987) *Readings in human–computer interaction*. Morgan Kaufmann, Los Altos

Barber, R. E., & Lucas, H. C. (1983) System response time, operator productivity and job satisfaction. *Communications of the ACM* **26** (11) 972–986

Bobrow, D. G., Mittal, S., & Stefik, M. J. (1986) Expert systems: perils and promise. *Communications of the ACM* **29** (9) 880–894

Carroll, J. M., & McKendree, J. (1987) Interface design issues for advice-giving expert systems. *Communications of the ACM* **30** (1) 14–31

Chin, J. P., Diehl, V. A., & Norman, K. L. (1988) Development of an instrument measuring user satisfaction of the human–computer interface. In: Soloway, E., Frye, E., & Sheppard, S. B. (eds) *Proceedings of CHI, Human factors in computing systems*. ACM, New York

Clarke, M. (1989) Explanations and the SIRATAC cotton management system. In: Quinlan, J. R. (ed.) *Applications of expert systems*. Addison-Wesley, Sydney

Cleal, D. M., & Heaton, N. O. (1988) *Knowledge-based systems: implications for human–computer interfaces*. Ellis Horwood, Chichester

Davis, R., & Lenat, D. B. (1982) *Knowledge-based systems in artificial intelligence*. McGraw-Hill, New York

Draper, S. W., & Norman, D. A. (1984) Software engineering for user interfaces. In: *7th International Conference on Software Engineering*. IEEE Computer Society Press, New York

Gardiner, M. M., & Christie, B. (eds) (1987) *Applying cognitive psychology to user-interface design*. Wiley, Chichester

Hartson, H. R., & Hix, D. (1989) Human–computer interface development: concepts and systems for its management. *ACM Computing Surveys* **21** (1) 5–92

Hill, I. D. (1983) Natural language versus computer language. In: Sime, M. E., & Coombs, M. J. (eds) *Designing for human–computer communication*. Academic Press, London

Houghton, R. C. (1984) Online help systems: a conspectus. *Communications of the ACM* **27** (2) 126–133

IEEE Software (1989) Developing human–computer interfaces. Special issue 6 (January)

Ince, D. (1988) Software prototyping and artificial intelligence based software tools. In: Kelly, D., & Rector, A. (eds) *Research and development in expert systems.* vol. V. Cambridge University Press, Cambridge

Lenat, D. B., & Feigenbaum, E. A. (1989) On the thresholds of knowledge. In: Quinlan, J. R. (ed.) *Applications of expert systems.* vol. 2. Addison-Wesley, Sydney

Mantei, M. M. and Teorey, T. J. (1988) Cost/benefit analysis for incorporating human factors in the software lifecycle. *Communications of the ACM* **31** (4) 428–439

Norman, D. A., & Draper, S. W. (1986) *User centred system design.* Erlbaum, Hillsdale, NJ

Otte, F. H. (1984) Consistent user interface. In: Vassiliou, Y. (ed.) *Human factors and interactive computer systems.* Ablex, New Jersey

Partridge, D., & Wilks, Y. (1987) Does AI have a methodology which is different from software engineering? *Artificial Intelligence Review* **1** (2) 111–120

Sell, P. S. (1985) *Expert systems — a practical introduction.* MacMillan, Houndmills

Shneiderman, B. (1987) *Designing the user interface.* Addison-Wesley, Reading, MA

Sparck-Jones, K. (1985) Natural language interfaces for expert systems. In: Bramer, M. A. (ed.) *Research and development in expert systems.* Cambridge University Press, Cambridge

Sutcliffe, A. (1988) *Human–computer interface design.* MacMillan, Houndmills

Wagner, E. (1988) *The computer display designer's handbook.* Chartwell-Bratt, Lund

Walters, J. R., & Nielsen, N. R. (1988) *Crafting knowledge-based systems.* Wiley, New York

8

The user interface: Computational models of computer users

Jason Trenouth and Lindsey Ford

8.1 REVIEW OF USER MODELLING

Modelling is an activity we all engage in, whether or not we are aware of it. Replacing a wheel on a car, for example, can only be successfully accomplished if we use some model of the various activities involved to inform us what to do next. Without such a model, however rudimentary, we could only throw up our hands in despair and await the help of someone with the required model. A model is an abstraction of some system or situation of interest that attempts to extract the relevant properties for the purpose of the model. A model is thus built with some purpose in mind, and its properties — the form and content of the information it contains — reflect that purpose. Our model for replacing a car wheel may have been built when first we watched someone else replacing their car wheel, or when we read how to do it in a car manual. In either case we would have built the model in order to use it ourselves in a similar situation, or to be able to use it in some other way — perhaps to help someone else. Such a model might contain the conditions under which it needed to be invoked — a flat tyre — as well as the sequence of steps involved in changing a wheel.

The model that has been referred to is a *task model*, i.e. a description at some level of detail (or abstraction) of the activities required to perform a particular task. If we were faced with the situation of needing to change a car wheel but did not know how to do it ourselves, i.e. we lacked the necessary task model, we may nevertheless be able to contact a motoring organization that could do the job for us. What enables us to take this action? We would in this instance be using some knowledge we have of the motoring organization. We know, for example, that its purpose is to give aid to motorists who have broken down, and that it will send a rescue vehicle to the site of breakdown. In other words, we are using a model of an organization to inform us what we should or can do. Our initial contact with the motoring organization — our expectations that we entertain about what the organization can do to help us — is dependent on our having a *system model* of the organization. Models such as these can be related to the design and use of computer systems. They have, furthermore, received considerable attention by cognitive psychologists.

First, however, we draw a distinction between software designers and software users. By 'software designers' we refer to those engaged in the design and development of computer systems. 'Software users', on the other hand, encompasses those who use the products of software designers. (Some people, e.g. software engineers, fall in both categories since they use software in order to design and develop software.) Software users draw from task and system models when engaging software. The system model encapsulates their understanding of what the software will do when they engage it, while their task model informs on how they engage the software in order to achieve their goals.

A software designer uses task and system models during the design process. There are two sorts of task model being used here. One sort represents the task the computer is to perform — and the builder must have a complete understanding of this if it is to find correct expression as a computer program — and the other represents those activities associated with the practice of software design and development. Furthermore, when the designer is developing interactive software, account is taken of software users, since without an awareness of the role they play, a product may be developed that is cumbersome to use and even unacceptable to the user community. The software designer must therefore take account of the models users may have of the product (users' system models) and the procedures users will need to apply when engaging the software (users' task models).

In most conventional systems, designers' models of users are implicit, i.e. they do not find explicit expression within the computer system. In recent years investigations have been made to embed explicit models within systems to enable them to be more sensitive to users. This development has encouraged researchers such as cognitive psychologists to pay greater attention to users' mental models. Fig. 8.1, based on Clowes (1987), shows the modelling activities that have been referred to. Johnson & Johnson (1988) have suggested that the user's task models may be further subdivided. Two categories they suggest are *system task models* which describe the set of tasks a system might perform to assist a user in achieving a particular goal, and *interaction task models* which describe the activities or behaviour of the person using the system to achieve the goal.

An example of a *system task model* is provided in Moran's (1981) Command Language Grammar (CLG), which gives a description of a system as the user sees it at six representational levels:

CONCEPTUAL COMPONENT	Task level
	Semantic level
COMMUNICATION COMPONENT	Syntactic level
	Interaction level
PHYSICAL COMPONENT	Spatial lay-out level
	Device level

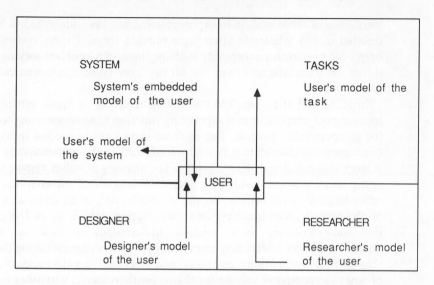

Fig. 8.1 — Types of modelling activity.

Within the conceptual component the task level describes the user's goals as a task hierarchy while the semantic level provides the task entities, or conceptual objects, that are involved in the task environment and on which actions are carried out. CLG can thus be regarded as providing a researcher's model of a user's model of a task.

With the exception of the system's embedded model of the user that has been briefly mentioned, the models discussed thus far are models created and used by people. An understanding of them has been necessary before an account of the model that is investigated in detail in this chapter, since this latter model is a reflection, or more correctly a model, of them. The model to be further discussed, moreover, is a model used by a computer.

'The computer as tool' has been a metaphor of long standing in computer science. However, another metaphor has emerged, not as a replacement for it, but rather one that better encapsulates the role of the computer in certain situations. It is 'the computer as agent', which attempts to convey the idea of the computer as a rational element of human–computer interaction. The metaphor finds expression in several branches of AI — namely, expert systems, ICAI and intelligent front-ends (IFE). An expert system, for example, contains a model of a human's problem-solving capability and expertise, and as such, users of it are dealing with an agent. An expert system would ideally also contain a user's task model and a user's model of the system as well as a problem-solving model in order to aid the user. The task model would aid its understanding of how the user perceives the task of interacting with it, and a system model would aid its understanding of how the user perceives what the system can do. Finally, it might contain a model of the individual traits of a user in order to communicate with the user in a sensitive and progressive way. However, although the need for at least some of these models in expert systems has been identified, it has not resulted in any wholesale attempt to provide them. Expert systems have been able to perform acceptably without them in a problem-solving sense, if not in a satisfactory way as far as user–system communication is concerned.

In ICAI and IFE, here too the system is acting as agent, either for an instructional purpose or in a supporting function to someone using software for an operational purpose. But in these instances the success in moment-to-moment communication is vital, in contrast to the expert system which is more concerned with eliciting only a few answers to well-defined questions and passing a single result to a user. The success of the communication relies largely, so we believe, on the system having at its disposal a model of the user. Unlike human–human interaction, which relies less on one individual knowing how another understands a task or system, human–computer interaction relies heavily on users understanding the tasks they are to perform using a computer, and users having a clear understanding of what the computer can do for them. Furthermore, a computer needs to have an understanding of a user in a deeper sense — his interests, motivations, background and preferred style of interaction, for example — in order to achieve the desired progressive understanding.

It is rare, though, that a system has explicit models of all three. Task and system models usually find expression implicitly, in ICAI systems at least, through the designer providing an interface engineered to meet his expectation of users' task and system models. If the designer's expectation is wrong, or if he fails to provide an interface to meet it, then we may be sure that there will be failures in communication. These will inevitably lead to interference in the learning process as far as ICAI systems are concerned, and ineffective use of software in IFE systems. Systems' embedded user models, or student models, are essential to ICAI since they minimally record a system's understanding of what the student knows, and this information is needed to determine what next action the system should take to foster learning on the part of the student. Without such knowledge a system is unable to individualize its teaching and thus cannot attain this particular goal of ICAI. It is rare to find embedded user models in IFE systems, on the other hand. However, we suspect this is due to the difficulty in building such models rather than a lack of their necessity.

In the discussion that follows we examine more closely the nature of systems' embedded models of users and how systems build them. The term 'user models' henceforth denotes such models.

8.2 A CLASSIFICATION OF USER MODELLING

8.2.1 Introduction
The aim of user modelling is to provide a computer system with information that will aid it in understanding the needs of its users. There are many types

of computer system requiring such an aid. These range from ICAI systems that are designed to impart knowledge to a user, through programming support environments, to complex applications software whose users need operational help, i.e. IFE systems.

Early programs for computer-aided instruction (CAI) merely scored students' answers. Students were given sets of problems to solve, the interaction proceeding on the basis of correctness of the answers (i.e. repeat with a similar problem set if incorrect, otherwise move on to the next topic). Little attempt was made either to work out why students answered some questions incorrectly, or to derive the student's current state of knowledge. However, with the application of AI techniques, particularly with respect to knowledge representation, it has become possible to model both the domain (of discourse) and the student more comprehensively. A milestone in this work was a system that used semantic nets as a means of representing knowledge about the geography of South America (Carbonell, 1970). Moreover, the application of AI has meant a shift from quantitative to qualitative modelling. Symbol processing languages such as LISP and Prolog have 'eased a move away from a statistical treatment of numerical measurements to a psychological interpretation of qualitative data' (Clancey, 1986). The result has been a considerable effort to provide such models but, alas, without a common vocabulary to describe them. The following is a means of classifying user modelling methods. The classification is mostly a synthesis of terms used in the papers on user modelling. However, some of the classifications can be attributed to the successive ideas of several authors. The indirect/direct partition comes from the ideas of Carr, Goldstein and Rich (1986); the individual/generic partition from Rich (1983); the functional/behavioural partition from Clancey (1986); and the buggy/ideal partition comes from Anderson, Boyle and Yost (1985), and Burton (1982).

We have purposely not used 'overlay' as one of the classifications. In the literature there is some confusion over what constitutes an 'overlay' model, and we found the term to be too general — as have others (Sleeman 1985). Instead a combination of several other classifications is equivalent to the original perceived definition, namely: explicit, extensional, dynamic, certain, representational, ideal and solid. Section 8.2.3 contains the definitions of these terms.

8.2.2 Structure

For simplicity and clarity we have chosen a 'question–choice' format. Questions are posed for relevant aspects of a user-modelling system and answers are given in terms of choices. We have tried to limit the choices to two; where a choice appeared to need more than two alternatives we subdivided the question if possible. Some questions have choices that are really points on a continuum. In these cases the choices given are the extremes. The choice points have been grouped according to three main topics: the model, the substrate and the dialogue.

8.2.3 Classification

8.2.3.1 The model
This first group of classifications is concerned with those attributes of the model itself.

Explicit and implicit modelling
Is the model inspectable or is it built into the system? If it is explicit then the model is real, tangible and open to inspection. The modelling is explicitly represented within the system. Most of the following classifications assume that the modelling is explicit. Conversely, if the model is implicit then the system reflects the model in the form of assumptions made by its designer. It is not inspectable, except perhaps as part of a design specification or through examination of the system's behaviour. Most conventional interactive software systems have implicit modelling.

Individual, stereotypical and generic modelling
Each user may be modelled individually in order to personalize the interaction. In ICAI such modelling of a student's knowledge is essential in order to determine the most effective next teaching action. For example see the TUTOR system (Davies *et al.* 1985). Alternatively, there may be one or more models of stereotypical users which reflect the properties unique to the stereotypes within the user population. A rudimentary system might merely distinguish novice and expert users, for example. GRUNDY is a prime example of a system that bases its reasoning on stereotype information (Rich 1983). Hybrid combinations of individual and stereotype modelling are also possible (see later in the KBET case study). A single generic model may also be used to hold common attributes of stereotypes.

Extensional and intentional modelling
Is the user model concerned with a current or a desired state of knowledge? In the first case the model consists of information about the user's current level of knowledge. It is concerned only with the user's present state (or extension). Complementing this approach a model may contain information about a desired level of knowledge for the user. It is concerned with a goal state (or intention) set by the user or the system. This latter classification is related to the study of plan recognition (Genesereth 1982).

Dynamic and static modelling
Does the user model change over time or is it immutable? The model may alter over time (in order to reflect some change on the part of the user or some change in a system's understanding of the user) or the model may be

fixed, so constituting an unchanging representation of the user (irrespective of any changes the user may undergo). The GRUNDY system is an example of such a static model (Rich 1983).

Active and passive modelling

Is the user model executable? The user model may be in such a form as to be executable, either by a known language interpreter or by a specially constructed one. The model can thus be used directly to simulate or emulate a user's behaviour. For example see GUIDON (Clancey 1982). Alternatively, the user model can be updated and queried but not executed. This type of model would be declarative in nature and, although it can still be used predictively, is not directly executable. For example see WEST (Burton & Brown 1982).

Predictive and non-predictive modelling

Is the model used to predict user behaviour? The model may be applied to predict the user's actions in a given situation (it may still be an active or passive model) or the model may not be used to make any predictions about the user. GUIDON and WEST are predictive and non-predictive respectively.

Retentive and forgetful modelling

Does the system remember the user model? The system may retain information about the user. Such models would be stored by the system for later reuse. Conversely, the system need not retain information about the user. In this case the user may be modelled individually at the time of each interaction, but this is not remembered in later sessions.

Weighted and certain modelling

Does the model cater for partial knowledge? Each item of knowledge in the model can have a weighting, i.e. a value associated with it which can be ordered with respect to the values associated with other items of knowledge. This includes 'probabilistic' modelling where the weights then lie in the range [0, 1]. It also covers the twin concepts of (1) how much an item of knowledge is believed to be known (by a student) and (2) what a system's confidence is in its belief that an item of knowledge is known (by a student). Conversely, each item of knowledge in the model can have one of two states — usually, 'known' or 'not known'. There may also be no information about an item of knowledge (a null state). Examples of both types can be found in UMFE (Sleeman 1985) and WUSOR (Goldstein 1982) respectively.

Representational and conceptual modelling
Is the knowledge representation scheme used as the framework for the model? This applies to (ICAI) systems that have embedded within them some knowledge base representing skills or information to be acquired by a student. The modelling may be done directly over the knowledge representation, i.e. the skills map directly onto the primitive elements in the knowledge representation. This is what is usually meant by the term 'overlay' (sometimes in combination with the classifications solid and ideal). Alternatively, the modelling may be done over a set of abstracted concepts, i.e. the skills map directly onto these concepts rather than onto the knowledge representation itself. For example see TUTOR (Davies *et al.* 1985).

8.2.3.2. The substrate
This second group of classifications concerns the substrate over which the modelling takes place. They decide the nature of the raw material that the modeller has to work with.

Cognitive and non-cognitive modelling
Is the user model based on a cognitive psychology of the user? This question can only be asked with respect to the substrate. Is it designed to represent a user's cognitive processes, such as Anderson's Geometry Tutor is claimed to (Anderson *et al.* 1985)? Most substrates are non-cognitive.

Behavioural and functional modelling
Is the model based on a description of action or interaction? The model may describe actions, i.e. the manifest behaviour of the modelled system. For example see GUIDON's substrate (Clancey 1982). Conversely, the model may describe the way in which processes interact with each other. It would give the functions of the components, and the overall behaviour of the modelled system would have to be derived from this functional description. For example see MACSYMA (Genesereth 1982).

Domain, reasoning and communication modelling
This point outlines the choice of substrates available to the modeller. The majority of systems that perform individual modelling only use the domain substrate, while others may model over the communication process. None that we could find proposed modelling over the reasoning process as distinct from any domain-specific reasoning methods.

Buggy and ideal modelling
Does the system model misconceptions? The user may be modelled over both misconceptions and correct conceptions, or may be modelled only over

correct conceptions. The prime example of the former type of system is DEBUGGY (Burton 1982).

Fluid and solid modelling
Does the system model over a fixed set of skills? The user may be modelled over a variable set of skills, i.e. the underlying knowledge that the system is modelling the user over may be changed by the system to aid the modelling process. For example, links may be added to a semantic net by the system in trying to model a particular user's associations. INTEGRATE (Kimball 1982) and QUADRATIC TUTOR (O'Shea 1982) are systems where the substrate is extended in the light of student activity, and are sometimes referred to as perturbation models. Alternatively, the user may be modelled over a fixed set of skills, i.e. the underlying knowledge that the system is modelling the user over is predetermined and unchanging.

8.2.3.3 The dialogue
This third group of classifications is concerned with the nature of the interaction/dialogue with the user.

Indirect and direct modelling
Is the modelling in the background or is it done openly? The model may be inferred from the user's behaviour. It would be done from behind the scenes while the user is engaged in some other activity, e.g. problem solving or information seeking. Alternatively, the user of the system may explicitly provide the modelling information, usually in response to requests for such information from the system. Examples are WEST (Burton & Brown 1982) and GRUNDY (Rich 1983) respectively.

Controlled and uncontrolled modelling
If the modelling is indirect, does the system have any control over the dialogue with the user? The system could prompt the user and direct the dialogue to some extent, i.e. the system is able to aid the modelling effort by making assumptions about the user input. Conversely, the system could have no control over the dialogue with the user, i.e. it is merely monitoring a dialogue the user is having with another system. GUIDON (Clancey 1982) is controlled and ANCHISES (Zissos & Witten 1985) is uncontrolled.

Atomic and compound modelling
If the modelling is indirect, how fine-grained is the modelling? Each interaction of the user with the system may be modelled. This style of modelling assumes that the dialogue with the user allows the step-by-step feedback that is needed. Alternatively, the modelling is done from the

interpretation of several steps, e.g. an ICAI system would work on the premise that the user may have used many primitive skills between successive parts of the dialogue. For examples see GEOMETRY TUTOR (Anderson *et al.* 1985) and DEBUGGY (Burton 1982) respectively.

Immediate and delayed modelling
If the modelling is indirect, does the system process each input to determine which skills are being used? The system may attempt to decide which skills are being used in each entry by the user. Alternatively, the system does not attempt immediate modelling on each input. Instead it draws conclusions about which skills are being used from larger samples of the input data — see for example ANCHISES (Zissos & Witten 1985).

Generation and statistical modelling
If the modelling is indirect and immediate, how does the system decide which skills are being used? Combinations of skills may be generated and the result of their application is compared to the user input for a match, i.e. a generate-and-test approach, usually beginning with combinations of only one skill and working upwards. This method combines well with atomic modelling, where only one skill is assumed to have been used. Alternatively, the skills may be discovered over a period of time by accumulating the results of the system–user dialogue. The modeller is told which skills might have been relevant to a given dialogue action, and successive actions illuminate those in use. This works best when the system prompts for a set of user replies whose skill content is likely to be 'orthogonal' or 'independent' in the same sense as the vectors of a vector space in mathematics. For examples see LMS (Sleeman 1982) and WEST (Burton & Brown 1982) respectively.

Structural and non-structural modelling
Does the system use the structure of the subject to help decide which skills are known? The system may be subject-directed in its updating of the model, i.e. the system's belief of the user's knowledge of one skill can entail a change in the system's belief about another skill, e.g. via prerequisite (or post-requisite) linking of knowledge in the subject. For example see WUSOR (Goldstein 1982). Alternatively the system may merely update the model solely on the basis of dialogue with the user and not use the structure of the subject to draw wider conclusions about the user's knowledge.

8.3 CASE STUDY

8.3.1 Background
The Knowledge-Based Engineering Training (KBET) project aims to produce a prototype computer-based system for engineering training using

knowledge-based techniques and interactive video. It draws on a variety of techniques from advanced interface design and ICAI and will result in:

- a demonstrator of a 'shell' for generic engineering training with a specific focus on aspects of computer numerically controlled (CNC) processes
- a kernel on which other applications can be built.

The way in which production is organized using CNC equipment varies in many ways and illustrates well the training requirements within high-technology engineering generally. In KBET we are representing generic engineering knowledge and specific knowledge relating to the operation of CNC machines. Coverage will be relevant to many aspects of production, including programming, setting and operating, tool selection, feeds and speeds, options with respect to auxiliary equipment (e.g. probes), safety factors and workholding.

Engineering knowledge is held in three forms: a knowledge base representing the concepts associated with the processes mentioned above; video stills and sequences exemplifying those processes; and a description of the stills and sequences. An individual frame, for example, may show several objects (a workpiece, a workholding device, a cutting tool, etc.). The video description will know about all these objects, where they appear on the frame, what their visual relationship is to each other (beside, behind, etc.) and on what other frames these objects appear.

Knowledge about the user is an essential component of such a system if it is to respond sensitively to him. Distinct types of end-user include training advisers, managers, production engineers, technicians and supervisors, instructors and lecturers, CNC-experienced chargehands and setters/operators, non-CNC experienced craftsmen, students, and users with no knowledge at all of engineering processes.

In KBET we are considering a wide variety of interaction styles and trying to map these onto the requirements of different users at different times. For example, an expert engineer may want to access a particular item of knowledge (in the knowledge base or as represented in a video image or sequence) and will need to be able to retrieve this with a minimum of fuss. The dialogue with a trainee operator, by contrast, may need to be highly managed, so that information is presented in a way and order that takes into account how the subject knowledge is structured and the current state of knowledge of the student.

The conceptual design of the communication system indicated a need for four dialogue decision-making modules, arranged in a hierarchy with respect to their distance from the user interface. There are also two information-providing modules that these draw on to make their decisions, namely the user modeller (UM), and the domain and video knowledge base. Fig. 8.2 shows the relevant part of the design of the user-modelling system. The lines between modules indicate the flow of control. The arrows denote the

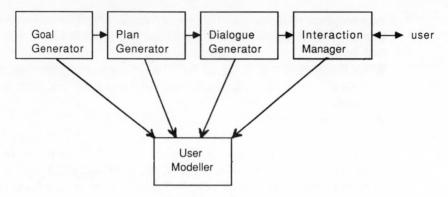

Fig. 8.2 — The KBET user modelling system.

direction in which it is passed — return of control being in the opposite direction.

The goal generator ultimately controls what may be several cycles of interaction. It generates a sensible goal for the particular user, based on information in the user modeller, which it then passes to the plan generator. This module determines a dialogue plan to achieve that goal, drawing on the UM to personalize it. This plan is passed to the dialogue generator which constructs the actual presentation, taking information to do this from the knowledge bases, and personalizing it by using the UM again. Finally, the interaction manager displays the presentation. Both the dialogue gener- ator and the interaction manager contribute event data to the UM, though that from the latter is finer-grained. Given the requirement for such an architecture and the necessity to allow for the variety of users mentioned above, the classification was applied to determine the characteristics of the user-modelling module.

8.3.2 Application of the classification

Each choice point in the classification scheme provokes analysis of the user- modelling requirement. We examine below each choice point with respect to the overall requirement of the system. Undertaking this exercise does not, of course, constitute the development of the user-modelling system, but it is informative on the critical decisions that have to be made with respect to it.

Concerning the model itself, it is clear from the outset that it is necessary to have an *explicit* user model that can be queried easily by the communication system. In addition, *implicit* modelling must be a non-starter for a self- contained user-modelling subproject. The *individual/stereotype/generic* choice point turns out not to be a choice at all. From the beginning it was envisaged that many different types of people would want to use the system: from qualified production engineers, through trainee technicians, to naive brows- ing users. It indicated the need for *stereotype* and *generic* mechanisms. However, it was also evident that *individual* modelling would be required if individualized training was to be accomplished. This led to the conceptual structure shown in Fig. 8.3, which envisages class inheritance. Now with each new user the system begins with a copy of a *stereotype* model rather than a blank template.

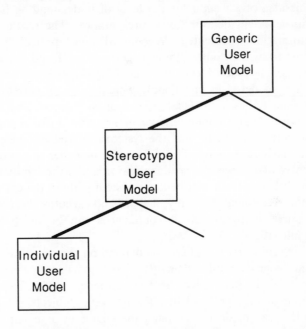

Fig. 8.3 — Conceptual structure of the model.

Clearly not all users, even of the same stereotype class, will have the same goals. They, or a supervisor, may wish to impose such goals, and the idea of *intentional* modelling is attractive. There is also a distinction between minimum and maximum goals, both for the user and for the supervisor. However, there is still a need to model a user's current state of knowledge in order to determine the extent to which a user's goals are being accomplished, and thus *extensional* modelling is also required. Of course, all the above discussion assumes *dynamic* modelling since an individual user's current and goal states of knowledge will change over time.

Although *active* modelling is desirable in problem-solving activities, since it allows for a more direct comparison with a user's actions, there was insufficient demand in the domain for this type of activity, and this allowed us to choose a *passive* model. As indicated in Fig. 8.2, the KBET system needs to predict the goals and plans that would best suit a user. This is a somewhat different idea, however, to a user-modelling system predicting actions of users, and to which the *predictive/non-predictive* choice point refers. There was no necessity to predict a user's actions, and a *non-predictive* method was thus adequate. For the next choice point, *retentive* modelling is obviously required since users may need to use the system many times and, for convenience, expect it to remember where they left off, what material they had previously seen, and so on.

We have a desire to measure a user's progress from current levels to goal levels. This introduces the notion of a weighting for a user's familiarity with the domain objects. In order to model the user over the knowledge base substrate, each domain object has associated with it a level of familiarity. This idea of a weight for the level of understanding has been integrated with a weight denoting pure presentation. The resulting weights are 'no information', 'presented', 'recognized' and 'applied'. The domain objects come from the domain knowledge base itself and are not constructed by the user modeller. Hence the modelling is *representational*.

The model is in fact doubly weighted. Each current and goal level of familiarity has an associated level of confidence. This arises both from a cognitive and a computational perspective. First, a confidence level is a measure of the belief that the system's inferences concerning the levels of familiarity are sound. This allows the modeller to reason about the confidences first to see if it needs to reason about the familiarities at all — thus paralleling a truth maintenance system without the complexity of backing up the reasoning. Secondly, it speeds up execution because the information required to reason about confidences can be much less than that for familiarities.

The substrate classifications depend on the structure and content of the knowledge base rather than on the user modeller. However, we can comment on a few of the choices here. The model itself is based on the abstract notion of an 'event' and an associated set of 'objects'. This is the basic input to the user modeller. Through the course of a session many such events would be generated and sent for interpretation. Here an 'event' is a description of a system–user interaction in a defined grammar, and an 'object' is a representation of any system object. The latter could be a domain concept, a particular piece of text, a particular piece of video, a video description, and so on. Because of this the user modeller will contain the information necessary to do both *domain* and *communication* modelling.

We did not include *buggy* knowledge (mal-rules, etc.) in the domain knowledge base since in the particular domain of tooling for CNC milling, for which most of our work was to be done, buggy knowledge consists largely of isolated incorrect facts that are not easily associated with correct conceptions. Instead we decided to adopt a more tutorial approach in which the user modeller would concern itself purely with *ideal* modelling, while the dialogue generator would interrogate the user during problem solving to recursively pinpoint and deal with the misconception locally. This is in contrast to a 'marking' approach where diagnosis is performed after the fact. (The classification has terms to describe the process, but see later.) Unlike the next choice, the UM shell does allow for easy extension in the direction of *buggy* modelling.

The user modeller does not augment the knowledge base substrate. That is, it performs *solid* modelling. To do otherwise would bind the modeller tightly to the knowledge representation scheme — something which we wished to avoid. In addition, the generation of such augmentation material introduces a new combinatorial explosion in the already difficult credit–blame problem.

The remaining choices in the classification concern the system–user dialogue. The *indirect/direct* dimension is elegantly dealt with in the KBET UM. The rules that reason from the event data to the levels of familiarity (see later) can cope equally well with either type of event. The decision lies with the communication modules, and here the events are mostly *indirect*. KBET definitely has some control over the dialogue, though how much depends on the current user model itself — hence it is *controlled* modelling.

The UM performs *compound* modelling. This means that more than one primitive concept may have been used during a dialogue act. Instead of the *buggy* paradigm mentioned above, the system performs *immediate* modelling. That is, it develops the model at each interaction rather than waiting for a large sample of events. The recognition of the use of skills or concepts in the user's dialogue is done *statistically*, i.e. the system's knowledge of the user's use of individual skills or concepts evolves over time. This circumvents the computational problem of generating and testing. Finally, the KBET modeller uses knowledge of the domain *structure* to augment its use of the dialogue to model the user. The following brief functional description of the KBET UM provides additional background material to the classification choices.

8.3.3 A brief description of the KBET user modeller
We can invert the incoming event data so that a set of events is associated with each object, i.e. as the modeller receives several lots of incoming event data, event histories can be created for each object. After each of these new events, rules can be applied to determine the new levels of familiarity. These rules can take account of event types and chronological orderings, creating a mapping from event histories onto current and goal familiarity levels. The following is a familiarity rule taken from the KBET user-modelling system:

> IF   THERE ARE RECENT EVENTS WITH Modes [recognized, recognized]
>
> AND   THE Reaction OF THE FIRST EVENT WAS correct
>
> AND   THE Reaction OF THE SECOND EVENT WAS correct
>
> THEN THE Current-Familiarity IS recognized

The variables 'Mode' and 'Reaction' are part of the structure for the event grammar. The full grammar contains variables for specifying 'Mode', 'Context', 'Complexity' and 'Reaction'.

If there are around fifty distinct events from the grammar, and if we keep an event history of only five old events for each object, then it means there is a need for a constant mapping of over three hundred million rules. Even allowing for gross contraction with suitably generalized rules, this is still going to be a large rule set. In addition, it will be rather slow to execute because of the need to search event histories. From a computational point of view we required a way of estimating whether we needed to invoke the familiarity rules at all. As we mentioned above, one way to do this is to implement a fully fledged truth maintenance system, i.e. backing up reasoning by premises, and when these become invalidated re-invoking the reasoning rules. Instead, however, for the sake of computational simplicity we introduced the notion of the system's confidence in its reasoned values. Then for the most recent event we can use a set of 'confidence rules' to determine whether this affects our confidence in the levels of familiarity. Thus only one event is being analysed by a resultingly much smaller rule base. These rules map an event and the current level of familiarity onto a change in confidence.

Now whenever the confidence strays below (or above) a threshold the full set of familiarity rules are invoked. How are the confidences initialized in the first place? Each of the familiarity rules has a confidence in its soundness which becomes the familiarity level's associated confidence level if that rule is fired. As an example, here is one of the confidence rules from the KBET system:

IF   THE Current-Familiarity IS recognized
AND   THE Mode OF THE CURRENT EVENT IS recognized
AND   THE Complexity OF THE CURRENT EVENT IS sequence
AND   THE Reaction OF THE CURRENT EVENT IS correct
THEN   THE Confidence-Change IS +2

With the addition of confidence information the earlier rule from the full familiarity rule set becomes:

IF   THERE ARE RECENT EVENTS WITH Modes [recognized, recognized]
AND   THE Reaction OF THE FIRST EVENT WAS correct
AND   THE Reaction OF THE SECOND EVENT WAS correct
THEN   THE Current-Familiarity IS recognized
AND   THE Current-Confidence IS high

The UM thus consists of two flat rule bases, one working only at the behest of the other. It has many other features — including stereotypes as initializers, unification of user histories and models, a simple forgetting mechanism, network propagation of dialogue events, etc. Further information can be found in a more detailed report (Trenouth 1988).

The reader can appreciate that much of the work on the user modeller has been completed. Our classification has undoubtedly helped us in this work; not only by providing a checklist of possible choices, but also by applying it, it indicated which of the many other systems we examined were relevant to our investigations once we had made our choices.

ACKNOWLEDGEMENTS

We wish to acknowledge the many other collaborators on the KBET project, including Brian Kriss, Reg Prescott, Rod Rivers, Chris Roast, David Seymour, Helen Tang and Chris Tompsett. Also we thank the Science and Engineering Research Council of the UK which funded the project through Alvey.

Finally, we both wish to acknowledge the support of our endlessly patient system administrator, Khalid Sattar, who has helped us enormously with Nroff (the text formatter) in particular and UNIX in general.

REFERENCES

Anderson, J. R., Boyle, C. F., & Yost, G. (1985) The geometry tutor. *IJCAI 85* Burton, R. R. (1982) Diagnosing bugs in a simple procedural skill. In: Sleeman, D., & Brown, J. S. (eds) *Intelligent tutoring systems.* Academic Press, New York

Burton, R. R., & Brown, J. S. (1982) An investigation of computer coaching for informal learning activities. In: Sleeman, D., & Brown, J. S. (eds) *Intelligent tutoring systems.* Academic Press, New York

Carbonell, J. R. (1970) AI in CAI: an artificial intelligence approach to computer assisted instruction. *IEEE Transactions on Man Machine Systems* **11** 190–202

Clancey, W. J. (1982) Tutoring rules for guiding a case method dialogue. In: Sleeman, D., & Brown, J. S. (eds) *Intelligent tutoring systems.* Academic Press, New York

Clancey, W. J. (1986) Qualitative student models. *ICAI Research Workshop 86*

Clowes, I. (1987) Alvey HCI Club User Modelling SIG, Logica Cambridge Ltd

Davies, N., Dickens, S., & Ford, L. (1985) TUTOR — a prototype ICAI system. In: Bramer, M. (ed.), *Research directions in intelligent knowledge based systems.* Cambridge University Press, Cambridge

Dede, C. (1986) A review and synthesis of recent research in intelligent computer-assisted instruction. *International Journal of Man–Machine Studies* **24** 329–353.

Genesereth, M. R. (1982) The role of plans in intelligent teaching systems. In: Sleeman, D., & Brown, J. S. (eds) *Intelligent tutoring systems* Academic Press, New York

Goldstein, I. P. (1982) The genetic graph: a representation for the evolution of procedural knowledge. In: Sleeman, D., & Brown, J. S. (eds) *Intelligent tutoring systems.* Academic Press, New York

Johnson, J., & Johnson, H. (1988) Practical and theoretical aspects of human computer interaction. In: Alexander, I. (ed.) *The world yearbook of fifth generation computing research and development.* Kogan Page, London

Kimball, R. (1982) A self-improving tutor for symbolic integration. In:

Sleeman, D., & Brown, J. S. (eds) *Intelligent tutoring systems*. Academic Press, New York

Moran, T. P. (1981) The command language grammar: a representation for the user interface of interactive computer systems. *International Journal of Man–Machine Studies* **15** 3–510

O'Shea, T. (1982) A self improving quadratic tutor. In: Sleeman, D., & Brown, J. S. (eds) *Intelligent tutoring systems*. Academic Press, New York

Rich, E. (1983) Users are individuals: individualising user models. *International Journal of Man–Machine Studies* **18** 199–214

Sleeman, D. (1982) Assessing aspects of competence in basic algebra. In: Sleeman, D., & Brown, J. S. (eds), *Intelligent tutoring systems*. Academic Press, New York

Sleeman, D. (1985) UMFE: a user modelling front-end subsystem. *International Journal of Man–Machine Studies* **23** 71–88

Trenouth (1988) Anatomy of a user modelling subsystem. Proceedings of the Third International Symposium on Computer and Information Sciences. Nova Publishers Inc.

Zissos, A., & Witten, I. H. (1985) User modelling for a computer coach. *International Journal of Man–Machine Studies* **23** 729–750

Subject Index

adaptive interface 138–139
ANCHISES 155, 156
ART 92, 95
artificial intelligence (AI) 27, 40, 45, 95,
   149, 151
   AI languages 95, 97, 100, 101, 104, 105,
      106, 107, 108

bench testing 16
buggy knowledge 154–155, 160

C 94, 95, 100, 104, 106, 107, 108
certainty factors 76–78, 160, 162
chaining
   backward 101–102
   forward 101–102
class variables 99–100
Cobol 107
cognitive emulation 61–63
command language grammar (CLG)
   148–149
computational psychology 45
computer numerically control (CNC) 157,
   160
conceptual model 28, 30, 32, 40
cost 18, 20
creep 20, 21
Crystal 95

database facilities 108–110
debugging 105–107
DEBUGGY 155, 156
demons 89
development environment 104–105
dialogue 143–144, 155–156, 158, 161
documentation 142

error handling 140
ESP Advisor 95
evaluation 14, 18, 144
expert system shells 42, 95, 97, 98, 100,
   102–104, 106–108, 111–112, 135

expert system tools 74, 92, 94–112
explanation facilities 110–111, 140–142
external interfaces 107–108, 140

feasibility study 61
frames 86–91, 92, 97–100
   active facets 88–89
   defaults 87–88, 98
   passive facets 87–88
   procedural attachment 88–89, 98

GEOMETRY TUTOR 154, 156
graphics 103–104, 108, 143
GRUNDY 152, 153, 155
GUIDON 153, 154, 155

help 142
human-computer interaction 134

inferencing 31, 101–103
   see also predicate calculus, deduction
inheritance 84–86, 98, 159
INTEGRATE 155
intelligent computer-assisted instruction
   (ICAI) 149–150, 151, 152, 154, 156
intelligent front-ends 149–150, 151
interpretation model 32–33, 60

KADS 61, 63
KBET 152, 156–163
KEE 92, 95
KL-ONE 96
knowledge
   conceptualization of 71–73, 60
   descriptive 71, 78–91, 92
   dynamic 30
   formalization of 71–72, 73–74
   heuristic 70–71, 74–78, 89–91
   identification 60
   static 30–31

Author index